# HOW TO CREATE
# FANTASIES
# AND
# WIN ACCOLADES

## A Practical Guide to Planning Special Events

## Doug Matthews

Order this book online at www.trafford.com
or email orders@trafford.com

Most Trafford titles are also available at major online book retailers.

Cover Design: Lee Edward Fodi
Cover Photography: Brian Arnold
Event Solutions Magazine, MH Concepts, and Visual WOW
Wayne Chose & Associates Photography
Cover 3-D CADD Drawing: Peter Neufeld Lighting Design
Cover 2-D CADD Drawing: Pacific Show Productions

Print information available on the last page.

ISBN: 978-1-4251-2802-9 (sc)

*Trafford rev. 03/05/2019*

 www.trafford.com
North America & international
toll-free: 1 888 232 4444 (USA & Canada)
fax: 812 355 4082

# Contents

# Preface

The industry called special events is changing – rapidly!!

From a few "party planners" and "entertainment agents" in the early 1980s to today's multi-national production companies and destination management companies, we have seen massive growth. As in any industry, this growth has come with its share of success stories and impeccably professional practitioners, and also with its share of failures and highly questionable ethics. It is an industry that has demanded the use and growth of technology, and it is an industry that has demanded the very highest levels of creativity from its practitioners. Fortunately, since those early years, the professionalism of the industry has grown, thanks to many dedicated individuals.

Throughout the 1980s and 1990s, the growth of special events paralleled the growth of the economy. Events became bigger and more expensive, corporations spent more to entertain their top employees and sales people, event marketing became a force in the corporate marketing mix, and public festivals became more elaborate. Indeed, it seemed as if the industry were bulletproof. We now know that was not the case. A series of almost simultaneous catastrophes - terrorist attacks, economic slumps in several countries, war, and disease - all served to knock the wind out of the fast-sailing special events industry. Suddenly, for event company owners and employees, it became more a matter of how to survive, not of how to best spend the excessive dollars of clients.

For those who did and do continue to survive, in many cases it now means that fewer people must do the job of many. Fewer people must now understand the complexities of special events. Fewer people must now create, organize the event, run the show, and pay the bills. For some companies, this may very well be the same person. If that person does not fully understand what comprises a special event and how to organize it, disastrous results are not far away.

Consider some of the following statistics found in the 2003 annual industry survey conducted by Event Solutions magazine[1] (includes all industry sectors - planners, services, caterers, rental companies, sites, technical companies, entertainment agencies and corporations), and my personal interpretation of the results:

- The average individual number of years in the industry was 13. This means that most people have seen only growth and have not had to deal with an economic downturn. It also means that most people have always had technology as a tool to help them.
- The average age is 43. This means that change may be difficult for people in this age bracket.
- The two biggest problems facing the industry were the economy (57%) and qualified employees (11%). This means that trained staff is hard to find at a time when the money to pay for their training or to hire them is not there.
- The average number of employees decreased by 28% between 2000 and 2001. This again means that there are fewer people to do the same jobs.
- The average lead time from date of order to date of event decreased by 8%, from 12.6 weeks to 11.6 weeks between 2000 and 2001. This means that more must be done in a shorter time.
- 81% of companies have their own web site sites but 54% of these did not redesign it in the last year. This means that there are a lot of companies out there who are going to miss out on the business to be gained by the Internet.
- 68% of respondents rely on the Internet either a fair amount or a great deal to do their jobs, and 76% could not do their jobs to a reasonable level without a computer. This means they are tech savvy, but it also means that they must keep up with technology and learn programs that may be foreign to them, like CADD, web site design, or others that might have been done by specialists in the past.

Where does this put us? It all means that to do business in this climate, individuals will have to change considerably: work for less, learn more about technology and specific industry software, and learn more about other people's jobs, simply to stay knowledgeable enough to keep clients, most of whom will continue to demand ever greater knowledge and creativity for their smaller budgets.

It is in this context that this book has been written. It is my intention to impart this knowledge in the form of a more in-depth examination of special events, with slightly more emphasis on private indoor events and their planning. The book is intended to apply to all special event planners from the novice to those in mid-career. It is organized in a manner that logically takes the reader from the initial concept of the event right through to the execution of the event. The layout is such that the sample forms may be easily copied for individual use or modified as needed. Indeed, I encourage readers to use these forms as templates for designing their own. The book is a "working guide" and not a hard cover esoteric work of non-fiction.

It should be noted that in the interest of political correctness, when required I have alternated the use of male and female pronouns in the book, in order to reflect the realities of the industry. This is in no way intended to favor one sex over the other.

My own career in this wonderful industry began 18 years ago when I walked into the office of Ben Kopelow, the then owner and founder of Pacific Show Productions based in Vancouver, British Columbia, and said I wanted to be a part of the action. Since then, I have had the pleasure of planning special events in Canada and in several locations in other countries, events that ranged from historic original theatre shows in the old gold rush town of Barkerville, BC, to stadium concerts, to corporate events of all types, to large public festivals.

When I started with Ben, computers were almost non-existent in business, the fax machine was barely starting to be used, and the Internet was beyond comprehension. We regularly hand-wrote proposals and gave them to our secretary (Yes, there actually were secretaries!) who typed them and mailed them to our clients. We waited about a week to ensure they had received them, then called and discussed the client's plans. Usually, a decision was made fairly quickly with not a lot of changes because it simply took too long to send all the information! What was even better, there was virtually no competition in what we did best, which was to create theme events at a time when they were a real novelty.

From there, things got faster, more expensive and more competitive. I happen to be someone who enjoys the challenges of technology so it became a pleasant undertaking for me to embrace computers and the Internet and all the promises they held. However, not all creative people are so inclined, and I watched many drop out of view. This was partly the reason for deciding to write this book, so that others would not be afraid to challenge themselves and learn about technology and the latest trends, thereby adding to the growing professionalism of the industry.

Throughout my career, I have, to put it mildly, had a blast. I hope that this book will encourage others to thrive and prosper in the industry.

# Acknowledgements

While a book is a visible compilation of thoughts and ideas, it is also an unseen compilation of encouraging words, suggestions from experts, lengthy discussions among colleagues, and occasional sleepless nights.

It is for the encouraging words, suggestions and discussions that I wish to gratefully acknowledge the following people:

- My wife, Marimae, for her patience and encouragement, not only in the writing of this book, but also as I painfully matured in this industry over the course of 18 years
- Mr. Ben Kopelow, the founder of Pacific Show Productions, and my mentor in the industry, for being hard on me and entrusting a huge knowledge base to my care, much of which I pass on in this book
- Ms. Julie Ferguson of Beacon Literary Services, for her extensive knowledge and suggestions on book writing and publishing
- My colleagues in TEAM Net, the Total Event Arrangements and Meeting Network, all of whom are skilled event producers in their own right, for sharing their knowledge
- Ms. Lynne Moran of Capilano College, for her continuing enthusiasm for my book as a useful addition to the texts of the college, and for allowing me to teach courses in event planning at the college
- Mr. Sonny Wong, of Hamazaki Wong Marketing Group, a friend and colleague, for sharing his knowledge of event marketing and sponsorship
- Mr. David Peake, of Peake of Catering, an award-winning caterer, for sharing his knowledge of catering
- Mr. Kevin Kay, of Clark's Audio Visual, a well-respected colleague in the A-V industry, for sharing his knowledge
- Ms. Lesley Corte, of Lesley Corte Designs, an unbelievably creative and enthusiastic décor designer who continues to inspire me
- My son, Stephen Matthews, of Q1 Production Technologies, for his assistance with

the lighting section
- Mr. Chris Briere, of Briere Sound, for his assistance with the audio section
- All the employees of Pacific Show Productions over the years who helped to create some wonderful fantasies
- Everyone else whom I may have missed but for whom I am truly grateful.

Thank you one and all.

# PART ONE

# ABOUT SPECIAL EVENTS

# 1

# What is a
# Special Event?

## DEFINITION OF A SPECIAL EVENT

A special event is a gathering of human beings, generally lasting from a few hours to a few days, and designed to celebrate, honor, sell, teach about, or observe human endeavors. Events, special or otherwise, have been around since prehistoric times, from that first buffalo kill and the accompanying feasting, to today's elaborate festivals for hundreds of thousands. In the distant past, they might have included coronations, human and animal sacrificial ceremonies, gatherings to pray to a variety of gods depending on the culture, the official opening and blessing of monuments, burials, battle victory celebrations, sports, and so on. In the recent past and today, they have come to include:

- Product launches
- Award and graduation ceremonies
- Opening and closing ceremonies
- Theme dinners and events
- Parades
- Festivals
- Sporting Events
- Concerts and theatrical presentations
- Exhibitions and trade shows
- Fundraisers
- Weddings and anniversaries

- Reunions
- Bar and bat mitzvahs and other cultural celebrations
- Funerals
- Meetings, conventions and conferences
- Speeches
- Dances
- Birthdays and children's parties.

Always in the background has been some sort of event planner or mastermind, albeit with varying and sometimes questionable skill levels. The "Wedding at Cana," the first miracle performed by Christ in the new testament of the Bible, in which he turned water into wine, and even the "Feeding of the Multitudes," another miracle in which he made five loaves of bread and five fish feed 5000 people, certainly lacked proper planning, especially in the catering department! The poor persons responsible would probably have been stoned to death had it not been literally for divine intervention!

Unfortunately, today we are not blessed with a godly assistant to cover our tracks so we must educate ourselves as much as possible to ensure there are no similar serious planning mistakes. This, of course, brings us to that Jack - or Jill - of all trades, the person who loves to be referred to as "god-like," the event planner.

# 2

## The Event Planner

### WHAT IS AN EVENT PLANNER?

Since what we know today as the "special events industry" has really only been around for about 20 years, even terminology is in the fledgling stage. Thus, an event planner is known by many names, and terms tend to sometimes be confusing and interchangeable. Basically, the most common terms are as follows:

### Event Manager

The event manager is the delegated representative of an entity that holds overall ultimate responsibility for the event. This could be the "owner" of the event, such as a company, city, non-profit organization (e.g. trade show, charity, festival, association), or even an individual. Usually, this person (event manager) also further delegates or sub-contracts other specialists in the many areas needed to accomplish the event. The event manager term is most often used in larger events, such as festivals or large event marketing events such as major sporting competitions (e.g. Molson Indy, Super Bowl).

### Event Planner

This term is sometimes used interchangeably with event manager but often tends to refer to those who plan smaller and more private events such as dinners, weddings, reunions, and similar gatherings. Frequently this is an individual operating independently, and not a company.

### Event Coordinator

Sometimes used interchangeably with event manager and event planner, this term tends to refer to an individual employed by a larger organization or a venue, who is responsible for bringing together all the event participants to ensure they are working toward the same goal. This person is usually not responsible for the creative side or supplier sourcing, but more for simple coordination duties. Examples can be found in convention centers and arenas that employ event coordinators to liaise with all parties engaged in creating an event.

## Event Producer

Sometimes used interchangeably with event manager and event planner, but most often refers to the person responsible for creating and executing the event, particularly the technical side that involves design, scheduling, staging, sound, lights, A-V, entertainment and décor. In the USA, a producer is more often associated with the audio-visual component of events.

## Conference and Meeting Planner

This is a specific area of expertise pertaining to the meetings industry and is generally more concerned with the functions and duties of arranging meetings such as organizing a call for papers, program setup, conference registration, badging, hotel accommodation and registration, plenary and breakout session organization, A-V arrangements, food and beverage arrangements, transportation, and various ceremony arrangements. We will not deal with this specific area in this book other than as some of the various typical conference events might relate to the topics at hand. There are many excellent reference books available on the subject as well as continuing education resources available through Meeting Planners International (MPI) and the Professional Conference Management Association (PCMA).

Throughout this book, we will refer to the Event Planner as the all-encompassing term for any of the positions defined above.

Increasingly in all cases, the individual must come to his or her job with more sophisticated skills than ever before. Although these to date do not require a university degree, the majority of persons occupying positions as described above, overwhelmingly hold at least a bachelor degree in some discipline, often closely related to the field, such as fine arts or drama.

# WHAT SKILLS ARE REQUIRED BY AN EVENT PLANNER?

The obvious benefits of an advanced - and continuing - education can be found in the skills now required by anyone wishing to pursue a career in special events. As we progress through this book, the requirements will become clear, as will the specifics of how and where to acquire them. For now, let us list the most common and most desirable skills and yes, even personality traits:

## Organizational Ability

A logical mind in order to keep a myriad of details, times, people, schedules, and tasks in their proper places.

## Creative Ability

A right brain orientation in order to conceive new ideas, which can be in conflict with the organizational or left side of the brain.

## Financial Acumen

A working knowledge of financial statements, basic accounting, and budgets.

## Writing Ability

A clear, concise, creative, and grammatically correct writing style is mandatory.

## Speaking Ability

A clear, organized, and enthusiastic speaking style is highly desirable.

## Computer Skills

Familiarity with the most used components of the Microsoft Office suite of software (e.g. Word, Access, Excel, and PowerPoint) is mandatory. Also desirable are familiarity with common customer relationship management (CRM) software such as Maximizer or Act, graphics software such as Adobe, CADD such as Vectorworks (especially in production), project management software such as MS Project, and finally total familiarity with the Internet, and desirably with web design.

## Previous Experience

At least some experience is desirable, even if gained by way of voluntary work. This helps to separate the huge number of potential job candidates.

## Personality Traits

Certain traits are almost essential:

- Gregarious and outgoing nature works best
- Upbeat, friendly and positive attitude, even during high stress times
- Ability to hide and manage stress and not get upset by it

- Flexibility in allowing changes to ideas and schedules
- Firm and fair management style.

As can be seen, there are widely varying skills and personality traits, a great many of which tend to clash with each other. It is a fine balance and can prove difficult for many job seekers who are not used to the constant pressures, late nights, high stress, changing client requirements and often low salaries. The rewards are high in terms of job satisfaction and that often compensates for the other less rewarding aspects.

# HABITS OF EFFECTIVE EVENT PLANNERS

Believe it or not, successful event planners do have much in common with each other. Over the years, I have come to identify several characteristic habits that they exhibit to achieve success. Although not every single planner is the same, here are some of the key habits:

## Focus

This is the ability to keep a specific event at the top of one's priority list. It starts with an understanding of the five main phases in the event planning process: Sales, Proposal, Organization, Execution, and Followup. Throughout each of these phases, the particular event must be at or near the top of a daily priority list.

## Anticipation

This is the single most important planner habit - in my own personal experience - that should be applied to every phase of the planning process, but most particularly during the coordination and execution phases. It is the ability to visualize the entire event from start to finish and to determine potential problems before they occur. To do this successfully requires a great deal of attention to detail combined with an ear that listens to the "little inner voice" telling you to be careful and correct this detail before something big happens; in other words, tuning in to intuition.

## Single-Minded Purpose

There cannot be any mixed messages in the mind of any of the event team members. This means that all those involved in the event - client, event manager/planner, producer, and all suppliers - must understand the goals and purpose of the event. The job of the event planner is to ensure that this happens. For example, if a planner has created a "Carnival Fun Night," it would be the responsibility of the planner to explain to the event team whether the goal of the event is just for attendees to have fun or if it is to build a sales team. Depending on the interpretation, two entirely different events could result.

## Ability to Devote the Necessary Time

Organizing events cannot be done piecemeal. Each phase requires a certain amount of dedicated time to complete and it is best to work on each phase all at once. For example, it is better to write a proposal over five hours rather than over five days, before moving on to the next task.

## Ability to Block out Interference

At first glance, this would seem obvious, but in today's harried work environment, it is not as easy as it appears. For example, when writing a proposal where creative thought is required, don't allow phone calls to interrupt your creative time. Either use an answering service or have someone in the office take messages. Another example, even more difficult to achieve, can be found onsite during event execution. In this case, try not to take cell phone calls (In fact don't even use the cell phone!), but rather ensure **all** the organizing is done prior to being onsite so all your attention can be directed to the successful execution of the event.

## "Show-Must-Go-On" Mentality

Every member of the event team, starting with the planner, must have this mindset. No challenge can be too big or too small. Being on time for everything is imperative. Performing in spite of hardships is a given in this business. Do what is promised when it is promised. Last but not least, keep a positive attitude to all staff and clients.

## Ability to Address Challenges

Everyone gets them, no matter how carefully an event has been planned. The main thing is to stay positive and pro-active. The second thing is to be fully aware of all the resources at your disposal and whether they can be used to solve a challenge/problem in a timely fashion. Lastly - and usually least - a planner should not be afraid to say, "NO!" if trying to make a change will compromise the quality of the event or the planner's reputation.

# 3

## How Are Events Organized?

### THE STRUCTURE OF AN EVENT

Events can be extremely complex as in the case of a major public festival or sporting event, or they can be simple as in the case of a wedding or a dinner and dance. Structurally, they all vary according to the amount of work the organizer wants to keep in-house and to the budget available for subcontracting.

In each case, an event planner may be brought in to handle some or all of the tasks of organizing the event. The amount of work the planner accepts and/or subcontracts will be dependent on his/her personal or company training and experience. Figures 3-1 to 3-3 represent some typical examples of simple, moderately complex, and extremely complex organizational structures for a variety of event types.

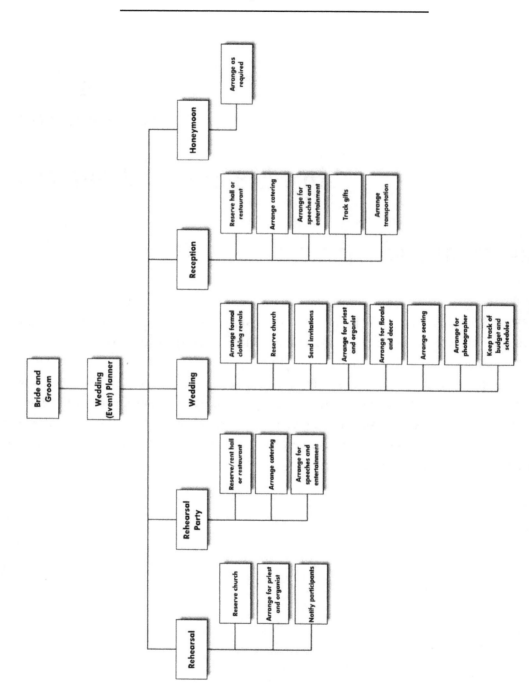

Figure 3-1: Example of a Simple Event Organizational Structure: A Wedding

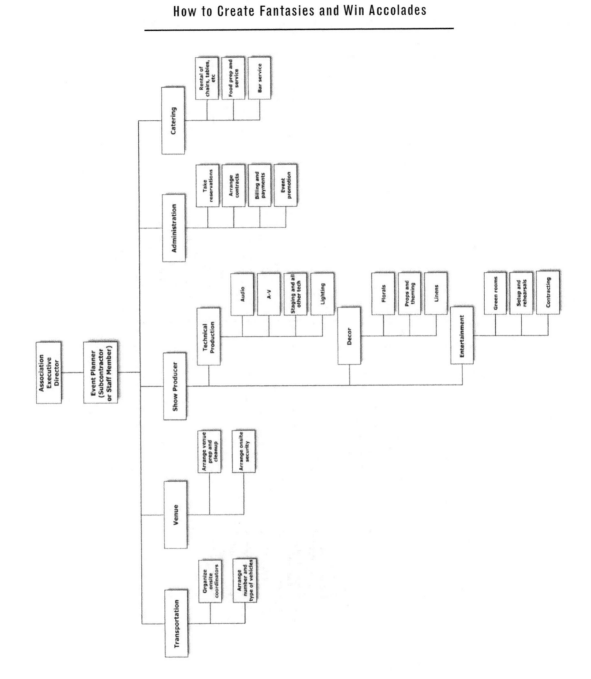

Figure 3-2: Example of a Moderately Complex Event Organizational Structure: An Association Theme Dinner at an Offsite Venue

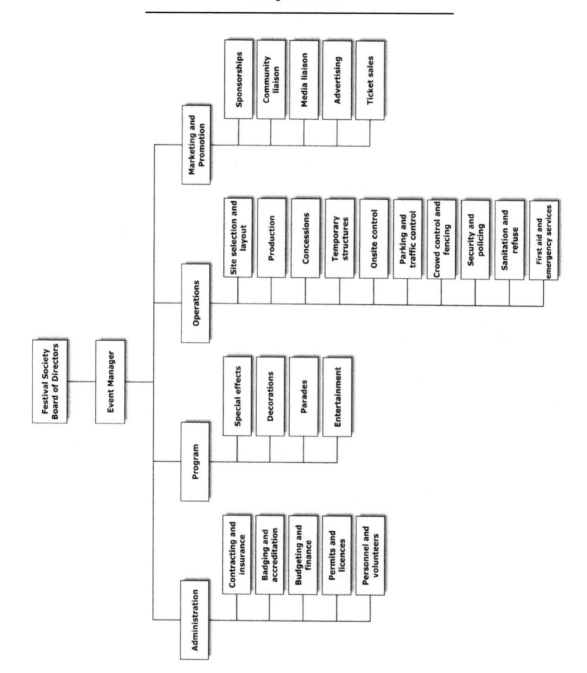

Figure 3-3: Example of an Extremely Complex Event Organizational Structure: A Festival

Obviously, before accepting or bidding on any work for these types of events, the planner must be intimately familiar both with her own capabilities and with those of suppliers and other resources that she might need to subcontract. Most planners tend to start small and graduate to the larger events, although many choose to stick with the niche that they know the best and in which they can pick up a significant market share of business.

Also, in considering what types of events to work on, the planner should be aware of the chain of command and exactly who she must report to, be responsible to, and get paid by. This is best determined before the work is accepted. Sometimes, for example, the work may seem enticing until the planner learns that a committee is in charge and that the entire process may be extremely frustrating due to constantly changing budgets and requirements. It may even be better to turn down this sort of work rather than face the frustration and many extra hours without additional remuneration.

Personalities can play a major role in the event management process as well. If at all possible, the event planner should determine exactly who she will be working for and try to meet with that person or persons beforehand. Strong-willed, hands-on personalities can often frustrate a knowledgeable planner due to unnecessary and usually unwelcome intervention by the client, making the entire planning process very stressful. A simple example might be an overly protective bride's mother who cannot allow the planner to make any decisions alone.

Budgets should be determined and obvious right from the start. The best and most efficient manner in which to manage an event is to know the exact budget before the work is even accepted. In that way, the planner can utilize the right suppliers and subcontractors to achieve the desired goals and not have to change suppliers at the last moment due to a reduced budget, although this sometimes cannot be avoided. The method of payment must also be known and agreed to prior to accepting the work and this must all be laid out in the formal contract (more to come about this).

Finally, the scope of work and responsibilities of the planner must be laid out clearly by the client before the work is accepted. Without this, it is too easy to miss something or let some item "fall through the cracks" thereby rendering all the planner's hard work useless. Again, this must be spelled out in a formal contract.

# EVENT EVOLUTION: THE PHASES OF PLANNING A SPECIAL EVENT

A number of event professionals have analyzed the event planning process and come up with just as many different ways of interpreting how it is done. I have chosen to break the process down into five main phases that mirror as closely as possible the logical steps that must be taken: These are:

## Phase One: Sales

The term "sales" can be interpreted in two different ways as it pertains to special events. Generally speaking, for private events (e.g. social, corporate, non-profit) and for the majority of events that the readers of this book will be planning, "sales" means selling their or their companies' expertise and services.

The second interpretation is that of selling the actual event itself, more in keeping with event marketing concepts, festivals, and major fundraisers in which sponsorships must be sold to help fund the event and tickets must be sold to attendees. Both these interpretations will be explained in detail.

## Phase Two: Proposal

In the event planning process, a proposal of some sort is invariably required in order to either secure a contract in the case of a private event, or to actually sell the sponsorships and tickets in the case of public events or major non-profit events. We will deal with each of these, considered to be the second phase in the evolution of an event, in detail.

## Phase Three: Coordination

Once the proposal has been accepted by the client or sponsorships begin to roll in, it's on to the next phase, coordinating, and organizing the event; probably the least enjoyable as it involves lots of detailed "grunt" work in the office. Nevertheless, it has to be done. In this phase, the event planner must exercise her abilities in a number of different management areas in different ways in both phases. Essentially, these management areas are:

- Risk Management
- Personnel Management
- Production Management
- Contract Management.

## Phase Four: Execution

This phase is the period that includes the event setup and the actual running of the event itself. Although we treat this and Event Coordination as two distinct phases, we will be discussing them together in Part Five of the book because they both involve different aspects of the same management areas outlined above, with the emphasis in the Event Execution Phase more on Production Management.

## Phase Five: Followup

The final phase in the evolution of a special event is that of followup. This phase begins the moment the event ends and involves analyzing the event's success or failure, adjusting any budget and contractual changes, thanking the client and/or participants, asking for an evaluation of the event, and last but not least, getting paid.

# Part Two

# Event Evolution:
# The Sales Phase

# 4

# What is being Sold:
# Selling the Planner's Capabilities

Depending where an event planner is in the "food chain" and depending on the type of event, there will always be an initial phase in which sales and the creation of a proposal must be accomplished. These break down quite simply into two different approaches.

For most private and corporate events, the planner is considered a subcontractor and must sell his services and capabilities to the potential client. This involves becoming known to potential clients and creating a sales and marketing plan for the planner and his company. Once a client is found and has expressed an interest in using the planner's services for an event, then a proposal must be created. This proposal is based on parameters usually outlined by the client, including a budget.

For other usually larger and often public events, the planner (event manager) has the task of selling the **event** rather than his capabilities. This type of sales and marketing comes in two forms, selling sponsorships to fund the event in whole or in part, and selling admissions to the event. The proposal in these cases takes the form of the event itself and how attractively it is packaged for potential sponsors and potential attendees.

In addition to sales and proposals, each event no matter which kind, must have a budget. This invariably forms part of the proposal and must be determined during this initial phase of the event planning process. We will deal with each type of sales and proposal separately.

This is undoubtedly the most common type of sales, in which the planner must sell to potential clients the capabilities of himself or his company. How is this done and what are the keys to getting sales? Here are a few tips:

- Keep a good database. Use a good customer relationship management (CRM) database such as Maximizer, Act!, or a customized version of a more sophisticated program like Microsoft Access. Categorize your clients into those who are repeat down to those you might not know but who hold good potential.

- Stay in touch with your clients, more so with those who are repeat, by means of direct mail, regular phone calls, and e-mails.

- Strive for referrals. Create a network of friends in the industry, both clients and suppliers alike, and strive to be well-known and respected so that your name is the first on their lips when they are asked, "Who is a good event planner?" Don't underestimate the power of referrals from suppliers.

- Follow up immediately on any leads that are given to you either by phone or e-mail or both.

- Create first class marketing material. This is a "glitzy" industry and it demands glitz in promotional material. Have an eye-catching business card and coordinated brochure.

- Create a web site in the same design as the rest of your promotional material. Have meaningful content and spare the fancy java script and other moving and noisy items. Use web marketing tools like pay per click or ensure you stay at or near the top of search engines by way of proper key words and meta tags.

- Become a member of key industry organizations such as MPI, ISES, CSES, PCMA, SITE, Board of Trade, and the Convention Bureau and strive to attend regular meetings in order to network.

- Form strategic alliances with other industry players either at home or further afield to broaden your reach.

# 5

# What is being Sold: Selling the Event

## WHAT MAKES A SUCCESSFULLY PROMOTED EVENT?

There are literally thousands of examples of this type of event found in today's exciting world of special events. Some of these include the Olympic Games, Molson Indy, PGA Golf Tournaments, Alcan Dragon Boat Festival, every kind of festival imaginable, and most fundraisers. Even weddings, bar and bat mitzvahs, or private dinner parties fall under this category because the organizer at the very least has to generate enough interest that guests will want to attend.

Whether your event is a charity fundraiser or a giant public festival, people will only attend if it meets **their** needs, not yours. This means that you must understand what your product is and how your potential audience views it. There are three main areas that must be addressed for the event to be successful, specifically with respect to selling sponsorships and more importantly tickets:

### Concept

What are you doing and why are you doing it? Has it been done before or has there been something very close done before? You may have a good idea, but if people perceive it as something that is not new, you will lose attendees.

### Location

Is it easily accessible by various means (car, rapid transit, walking) and easy to find? Does the location match the concept (i.e. If it's a high-end charity fundraiser in a low-end hotel, there is not a match)?

## Date

What else is going on at the same time in terms of conflicting demands on the potential audience? Does the concept fit the season (i.e. Is there too much entertainment on outdoor stages in the middle of winter)?

For the larger ones with which we will be concerned for purposes of this course, the selling takes two forms: selling sponsorships to fund the event and selling tickets to attend the event. Here are some general comments and guidelines for both forms.

# SELLING SPONSORSHIPS

This enters the complex realm of "event marketing" in which an event is used as a major form of marketing for a company. This is an advanced and very specialized area of marketing usually handled by advertising agencies or public relations firms. Typically, the amount of sponsorship is related to the extent of public exposure and advertising that the event is willing to give the sponsoring company. A good and very obvious example is the television rights for the Olympic Games that are worth millions of dollars to the Olympic organizers. In turn, the TV networks can pass on this exposure to their advertisers and generate income themselves.

Why sponsorship? Sponsorship has a proven return on investment (ROI). Studies have shown that sponsorship closes the gap in purchase likelihood. In other words, people who attend an event with a sponsor are more likely to buy from that sponsor than they are from a company who is not an event sponsor. It is only logical considering that the plethora of media options available today has reduced the effectiveness of general advertising. As a result, sponsorship in North America is growing considerably faster than advertising or general sales promotions.

Sponsorship brings the sponsors directly together with their target market and in so doing has several potential benefits:

- Increases sales
- Establishes or maintains a good public image (e.g. environmentally friendly or charity-conscious)
- Increases product and company awareness
- Builds relationships
- Increases employee motivation and productivity
- Blocks the competition.

How do you sell to sponsors and how do you keep sponsors happy? This is very different from selling to potential private clients as in the first method outlined above. This method involves much more thorough research. Key points to consider include:

- Review and research potential sponsors, especially ones who are known to be friendly to this type of marketing.
- Understand and research the potential sponsor's target market, including reading annual reports.
- Approach them early and understand when and how they should be approached.
- Create a totally professional and creative proposal and sponsorship package (see below).
- Try for a face-to-face presentation.
- Document all commitments.
- Establish only one contact person for all sponsors.
- Set up a good communication system for sponsors using newsletters, seminars, sponsor area on your web site, special VIP area on-site to accommodate them and their needs.
- Recognize and thank your sponsors whenever possible.
- Evaluate sponsorship results by:

  o Developing a measurement system for sponsor activities,
  o Gathering data from sponsors by interviews and surveys,
  o Including sponsor-related questions on event surveys, and
  o Collecting media clippings to prove the extent of event coverage.

## SPONSORSHIP PACKAGES

Creating a package that has value to the sponsor is the key to successful sponsorship selling. Every event is different, but there are always some elements of the event that do have value, including such items as:

- Radio, TV, and print partners
- Retail outlets
- Collateral material (e.g. posters, flyers, brochures, table tent cards, event programs,

envelop stuffers)

- Banners
- Tickets
- VIP seating
- VIP parking
- Hospitality suites
- Event signage
- Trade show booths and exhibits
- Onsite audio announcements
- Billboards
- Product sales and displays
- Celebrity appearances and tie-ins
- Internet exposure and links.

Of course there are many more opportunities that will be limited only by your imagination and the parameters of the event itself. Take the time to explore all opportunities in depth and to brainstorm all the possibilities with your event team.

The actual levels of sponsorship will depend on what you have brainstormed for the various sponsorship opportunities and how these have been applied to what you would consider reasonable levels of funding that you require for your event.

What follows on the next page is a hypothetical sponsorship package developed for a hypothetical public festival. Let's call it the Rain Forest Festival since this is being written in the heart of Canada's west coast rain forest. It will be an outdoor, spring event with a goal of attracting family audiences over a two-day period and will be in a large public space easily accessible by car and public transit.

Table 5-1: The Rain Forest Festival - An Annual Celebration of West Coast Entertainment and Culture

## Sponsorship Opportunities

| Opportunity | Title Sponsor | Platinum Sponsor | Gold Sponsor | Silver Sponsor | Bronze Sponsor | Friend of the Forest |
|---|---|---|---|---|---|---|
| **Dollar Value** | $100,000 | $50,000 | $25,000 | $10,000 | $5,000 | $1000 |
| Name and logo with title of event | X | | | | | |
| Name and logo on all paid advertising (Print, TV, radio) | X | X | X | | | |
| Name and logo on all paid advertising (Print only) | | | | X | X | |
| Name and logo on all event programs | X | X | X | X | X | X |
| Prominent booth or display space at event | X | | | | | |
| Display space at event | | X | X | X | X | |
| Name and logo on all event tickets | X | | | | | |
| Name and logo on Main Stage | X | | | | | |
| Name and logo on primary event signage | X | X | X | | | |
| Name and logo on secondary event signage | | | | X | X | |
| Complimentary parking | X | | | | | |
| Hospitality passes | X | | | | | |
| Celebrity talent access | X | X | X | | | |
| Complimentary event tickets | 24 | 16 | 12 | 8 | 4 | 2 |
| Product sales program with sponsoring media | X | X | | | | |
| Access to contact list for marketing | X | X | X | X | X | X |
| Acknowledgement plaque | X | X | X | | | |
| Acknowledgement certificate | | | | X | X | X |

# SELLING TICKETS

For any public event small or large, there will invariably be a component of ticket sales that can be either quite basic and involve a simple ticket booth, or very complicated and involve computerized operations and Internet ticketing.

Although we will not go into a detailed examination of ticket selling operations, some of the event planning considerations for tickets sales include:

- Pricing in relation to the expected demographics of attendees (e.g. family discounts, seniors, children)
- Pricing in relation to overall budget and revenue needed to break even, venue size and expected audience numbers
- Single event or multiple events on multiple days
- What the market will bear in pricing
- Staffing required for ticket sales onsite and in advance, including ticket takers
- Feasibility of Internet sales and the cost
- Type of tickets (e.g. electronic, hard, roll)
- Types of sales (e.g. cash, credit card) and the internal control required for each
- General admission and/or reserved seating, including the need for ushers
- Complimentary tickets
- Possible requirement for ticket-taking machinery and booths, including possible cover if outdoors
- Feasibility of using a professional ticket-selling agency.

Finally, how does the planner get the word out to potential attendees that this event is going to be the greatest must-see spectacle to come along since the parting of the Red Sea? In other words, how does one advertise the event? Here are a few ideas that seem to work for most organizers:

## Public Service Announcements

Otherwise known as PSAs, these are brief free advertisements placed in local newspapers and on radio and TV explaining the specific details about the event. They are quite easy to acquire if the event is charity-driven, not so easy if it is for profit.

## Direct Mail

A letter from the organizers announcing the event and the benefits of attending can be a good mail out piece. This is best used with a targeted audience of previously known supporters of the cause if there is one, or to a mail list of potential attendees with the demographics of the targeted audience. The letter should state where and how tickets may be purchased and the cost. A corresponding discount that favors the letter reader should be considered.

## E-mail

Often today this is a very efficient method to send regular reminders to a targeted market, especially if a direct link to a web site is available within the e-mail where one may purchase event tickets online.

## Posters in Key Locations

Anywhere where the target audience may visit is a good location provided that approval is granted by the owners of the location.

## Newsletters

Industry or organization newsletters can be an excellent way of priming potential attendees, especially if excitement for the event is built up over an extended period of time.

## Tying in With Sponsors

Perhaps there are locations where your sponsors have stores that you can tie into with brochures or small point-of-purchase advertising.

## Press Releases

A regular series of press releases timed to build up to the event can create excitement. Maintain regular contact with media and treat them well and respectfully.

## Paid Advertising

Always possible but of course this is the most expensive way to go. Possible locations include public newspapers, TV, radio, transit shelters, billboards, industry magazines, and other publications.

Basically, a coordinated campaign of advertising timed to lead up to the event is the most successful method of attracting potential attendees.

# Part Three

# Event Evolution:
# The Proposal Phase

# 6

# What Constitutes
# a Good Proposal?

In the two types of sales outlined previously, a creative and professional proposal is the key to a successful sale.

In the case of the typical private or corporate event, once the planner has prospected a lead and that lead or potential client finally asks for a proposal, the planner has to be prepared to go into action in a number of different ways. First, she must know the right questions to ask in order to even begin the proposal and second, she must have a wealth of knowledge and suppliers within easy access in order to create the proposal in a timely fashion. We will go through the entire process in detail shortly.

In the case of a larger public event - or even a fundraiser - the proposal takes the form of sponsorship packages and event advertising as explained in the previous section. However, whether the event is private or public, the planner or event manager still has to create the event itself and it is in the proposal phase that this creation takes place.

Thus, although emphasis in this book is on planning a private event, many of the same principles and categories apply as for a public event for which tickets and sponsorships will be sold.

## PREPARING A PROPOSAL

Without question, this is the most important phase of the event process. It is in this phase that all the creativity and budgeting takes place. It is also in this phase that your reputation as a creative planner is made. Without a successful proposal, there can be no sale. The planner must do most of the research for the event during this phase and often must work to very tight deadlines, so the true test of one's planning, creativity, and organizational skills is passed or failed here.

# WHERE DO THE IDEAS COME FROM?

Now that you must create that fantastic event proposal to "blow away" the competition and enthrall your client, how is it done? Where and how do you get those great ideas? The basic ingredients of a fantastic special event, no matter how complex, and the accompanying proposal, are really quite simple:

## Establishing the Event Parameters

This very simply means asking the right questions of the client as well as understanding the goals and reason for the event. The best time to do this is naturally right at the start when either you have been asked by a potential client to prepare a proposal - as a result of your sales efforts - in the case of a private event, or must put together a sponsorship package for a larger public event or fundraiser.

## Coming up with the Creative Ideas

Nowadays, a creative concept is absolutely essential to winning most business. Knowing how to apply the creative process to event planning can lead you to some very wild and wonderful new ideas, but you have to have an intimate knowledge of the resources at hand.

## Preparing the Budget

Budget considerations are part of every proposal. Knowing how to charge for your services so as to incur the optimum profit yet still give the client value for their money is a key ingredient of a successful proposal, so much so that we have devoted Chapter 7 to this topic.

## Understanding the Ethics of Proposals

When the special event industry was in its infancy 20 years ago, nobody worried about ethics. The possibility of having one's ideas stolen was not a consideration, nor were the many other "foggy" areas of business ethics. They definitely are today and it behooves the event planner to protect herself. Chapter 8 is devoted to this topic.

## Putting it All Together

How do you effectively combine the creativity, resources and budget?

## Preparing the Proposal Itself

How should it look? How should it be worded? What should be included? These are some of the many questions that must be considered to prepare an effective proposal.

## EVENT PARAMETERS: WHAT ARE THE RIGHT QUESTIONS TO ASK IN ORDER TO PREPARE A PROPOSAL?

The planner may only get one chance to dialogue with the potential client and therefore all the right questions must be asked at that time. As a minimum, at least the following must be determined at this time:

### Client Details

Name, company or organization, company address, phone and fax numbers, e-mail address.

### Event Details

Date, time, location, number of attendees, ages, background.

### Venue Details

Address, room, contact name and number, setup and strike times, what is happening in or near the room before and after the event.

### Specifics

Past similar events that were successful and why, past unsuccessful events and why, décor ideas or themes, entertainment ideas or themes, A-V requirements, special staging requirements, speeches, budget or at minimum a budget range, and date proposal is due.

It is a good idea to put all the necessary questions on a form for handy reference when a potential client finally does ask for a proposal. It can make the planner appear unprofessional and disorganized to have to return to the potential client to ask simple questions that were not covered at the first opportunity. A typical Sales Lead Sheet is enclosed as Sample Form 6-1.

Sample Form 6-1: Sales Lead Sheet

Date:_____

Name: _____

Company/Organization: _____

Address: _____

Phone: _____Fax: _____E-mail: _____

Best Time to Call: _____

Type of Business: _____

Event Details: _____

    Date(s): _____Location(s): _____

    # Attendees: _____Ages: _____

    Show Time: _____Show Length: _____

Approx. Budget: _____

Entertainment Priorities: (e.g. Name act, dance band, floorshow, variety act, ethnic performers)

Decor Priorities: (e.g.: Specific theme, props or design needed, etc.)

Other Details: (e.g. Who have you used in the past, other needs like sound, lights, staging, etc.) or Destination Services (e.g. Transportation, tours, hotels, etc.)

Promo kit sent:    YES_____      NO_____

Date sent:_____

Deadline Date for Proposal: _____

# CREATIVITY

Creativity is a wonderful tool and an absolutely essential one in the special events industry. People often enter the industry believing they are logical and organized and therefore will make good planners. Unfortunately, a good planner must be well rounded and able to draw on her creative juices when required. Although it is possible to utilize other staff or suppliers for this creative process, they are not always instantly available for a short lead-time proposal. The good news is that, with practice, just about anyone can be "creative."

One should understand that creativity, like many other human activities (e.g. writing, driving, and reading) is an acquired skill and not necessarily a gift with which one is born. As such it can be learned; however, like those other skills, it must be practiced. For some, such as those with a so-called left-brain, logical orientation, it might require more practice than for someone with a right-brain orientation, but it is possible to achieve a high degree of ability.

The process or "skill" of creativity has several key elements:

## Quantity Equals Quality

Although there are those who subscribe - with some proof - to the belief that one's first idea is usually the best, in the case of creativity, the first idea usually becomes a lead-in to even more and better ideas as the first idea becomes the building block for the ideas to follow. The point here is that one should not stop at only a few ideas, but rather continue to exhaust all possible avenues of ideas within a given theme. Writing them down and brainstorming with colleagues is the best way to get the most ideas.

## Suspending Judgment

Nothing kills creativity more than a phrase like, "If it ain't broke, don't fix it," or something similar. All those participating in the creative process should understand from the outset that pre-judging an idea can not only cause that idea to be lost forever, but it can also cause it's creator to become discouraged with the process and with the detractor. Never let judgment into the creative process.

## Relax and Have Fun

After "playing" and practicing with creativity for some time, one usually finds that the creative process is best served away from the daily work environment, often when the brain is relaxed. Some of the more successful environments to achieve this state are:

- During sleep (or rather "near-sleep"). Don't be afraid to keep a pencil and paper beside your bed and jot down ideas during the night. In fact, if the ideas do start to form freely, avoid the temptation to force yourself back to sleep and continue with the process until you have exhausted all possibilities in that particular line of thought.

- During a favorite relaxing activity. Massage, meditation, listening to music, reading, and taking a sauna are all relaxing activities that tend to free the brain from unwanted clutter and stress. In turn, you are more able to conceive ideas and take them to their logical conclusion.

- During a favorite aerobic activity. As long as it is not overly strenuous, this is one of the best ways to get the ideas flowing. Not only does this increase blood flow to the brain but it also releases endorphins to aid in relaxation. In combination, this can be very powerful in generating new ideas and working them through to conclusion. Examples are walking, swimming, and cycling. Note that the activity should be for a minimum of about 30 minutes or more.

## Lateral Thinking

Popularized by Dr. Edward De Bono[2], this concept is one of the most useful methods to force the mind to think "out of the box." In its most basic form, it simply takes an unrelated thought or item and force-fits it back to the related topic in a new and different way.

For example, if you are trying to develop some creative ideas for an event that will exemplify a conference theme of "Striving to Greater Heights in the New Millennium" at a theme dinner, including décor and entertainment, you may choose a random word such as "refrigerator" and try to force fit an association with the theme in a logical progression. The process might go like this:

- "Refrigerator" leads to
- "Cold" leads to
- "Cold air up high in the atmosphere" leads to
- "What is up high?" leads to
- "Planes/balloons/satellites/spaceships" leads to
- "Looking down on the earth" leads to
- "Looking down on the past years" leads to
- "Series of photos" leads to
- "Close-up aerials changing to satellite photos of earth" leads to
- "Equating to past performance" leads to
- "Maybe old time flying machines progressing to modern flying and the space shuttle"

leads to
- "Could reflect in variety of table centers and décor",
- "Could also reflect in entertainment story and dance",
- "Could reflect in A-V."

The best way to achieve results with this process is to maintain a list of random words that can be used as "idea generators" and starting points for the process of "force-fitting" to get to the idea that will be associated with the event itself, or some component of the event.

## Practice

Nothing improves creativity more than practicing it on a regular basis. Challenge yourself at every opportunity and keep the ideas flowing for every event, no matter how small. Remember, it is like any other skill and it needs to be honed or it will be forgotten.

The creative process as explained and applied here is best done in conjunction with an extensive knowledge of resources so that once the ideas come, they can be mixed with the various resources at one's disposal, and thus the great new ideas will flow.

Because resources are so important to event planning and indeed, basically **are** the event, we will devote Part Four of this book to them, with explanations in detail so they can be understood as much as possible.

# ABILITY TO PUT IT ALL TOGETHER

Once you have all the resources gathered and the overall event plan and/or theme in place, how do they all work together? What is the "flow" of the event? Do you use entertainment in between courses or only after dinner? Do you lead people from one place to another? How do you combine speeches and other event elements (dinner, dance, stage show, parade, awards, etc)? This is really only limited by your imagination and of course, the budget, although budget should not impact how the event flows. The key things to remember in planning how to make the event work for you and for the guests are:

## Be Aware of Three Dimensions and Scale

Try to use the entire event space to best advantage. Remember that we exist in three dimensions and that using those dimensions as much as possible will make the event more impressive. Consider tall props or décor elements that hang from the ceiling and use lighting on all walls, floors and ceiling. Remember floors and ceilings as much as walls. Fill the space and also remember that bigger is generally better when filling space.

## The Element of Surprise is Powerful

From the immediate gasps as guests enter an event to the congratulatory comments after it's over, plan for the unexpected in order to win your audience. Always have a surprise up your sleeve.

## Timing is Everything

Strive for a "seamless" event with no pregnant pauses. One element should flow smoothly into the next and it should all appear natural, as if it were not planned but just magically came together (Of course you sweat bullets to ensure everyone is at the right place at the right time!). Always prepare for the next planned element, such as a dinner course, well in advance.

When putting your creativity to the test by combining all those spectacular resources, you will need the inspiration of your suppliers as well as your own. To use them most effectively, ensure that they are totally up to speed with all the ideas you have and with your plans and what the venue will allow them to do in their areas. Everyone has to have the same goal in mind to achieve the best coordinated event.

Try to have fun and enjoy the creative process and the opportunity to actually create something new and different. Try to convey this sense of exuberance to your client in the form of your proposal.

# PREPARING THE PROPOSAL ITSELF

The actual proposal is your own unique stamp and brand. The way it is presented and laid out is what sets you distinctly apart from your competition. There is no right or wrong way, but based on experience, here are several tips:

## Layout

Style is your own; however, besides style, grammar, spelling, and punctuation must be absolutely perfect. There is no reason in this age of computer spell-checking that a proposal should not go out perfectly written.

## Format

Although some clients may appreciate and even encourage a format that is a little "over the top" in terms of creative presentation, it has been our experience that succinct descriptions of items in a "shopping list" format seem to work the best. A description that creates a visual picture is good as long as it does not get too verbose.

## Technology

If at all possible and budget permits, definitely use technology. This can include two or three-dimensional CADD - or even hand-drawn – colored renderings of the event or a main component of the event (e.g. décor or stage), photos of past similar events, and videos in a compressed format. Current technology allows you to design an event space in 3-D and then actually "fly through" the room, entering it and viewing it exactly as a guest would see it! You may even want to consider burning the entire proposal onto a CD or DVD complete with a composite video of all the entertainment and décor ideas in photographic form. Cheap and easy-to-use video editing software is now available for home or office use, making this possible at very low cost.

## Delivery

Although regular mail is still around, the norm for the event industry has definitely switched to e-mail. If you send your proposal by e-mail, you should ensure that you have the latest anti-virus software that checks your **outgoing** e-mail and attachments for viruses before sending, in order to protect your client. Obviously, you need to include the proposal and likely additional photos or even the compressed videos; however, if you do send photos or videos, out of courtesy let the client know that there will be a large file coming (first check that the client has high speed Internet access). If you send these you should also consider "zipping" them first to decrease the file size. Lastly, ensure the videos or event audio files are in a format that can be read by the latest windows media player, as that is the most common player on the market and almost everyone with a PC has the player.

## Timing

Be prompt in replying to the proposal request. Submit it on or before the target date and don't forget to follow up within a few days of sending it to ensure it was received in good order.

Sample Form 6-2: Proposal Phase Check List

This phase begins when the potential client asks for a proposal, whatever size or type the event is. Tasks include:

- ☐ Set date for completion with client.
- ☐ Take time to develop concept, think of ideas, and create.
- ☐ Determine overall event budget, then set budget for each component after deducting your own profit margin.
- ☐ Call suppliers, such as decorators, performers, tour operators, audio, and lighting companies for quotes.
- ☐ Ensure all necessary taxes are included in supplier costs.
- ☐ Give suppliers time to prepare their proposal and give them a target date. Stick to it.
- ☐ Ensure suppliers' creative time is included in proposal as a line item.
- ☐ Include your own time for event coordination as well.
- ☐ Type up proposal in creative format. Use visuals and lots of description if time permits. Keep budget separate on a summary page or type line-by-line.
- ☐ Spell-check proposal and double check for grammar.
- ☐ Check for correct client name and address.
- ☐ Put copyright page after title page.
- ☐ Include promo, tapes, and videos where needed. If decor is a big part of proposal, try to use color-printed or copied, customized, titled pages with pictures. At a minimum, try to include an artist rendering or sketch of new decor with the proposal. Put the sketch or rendering on a titled page.
- ☐ E-mail/mail/courier/fax proposal to client.
- ☐ Call client the next day to ensure proposal was received.
- ☐ Call client every two weeks to check on progress.

# 7

## Budgets

Let's not beat around the bush. To be successful in preparing proposals, an event planner must know his profit margin intimately. It is this and really only this that determines how you will charge for your proposal. Several factors are important in calculating the budget and how you will charge:

- How will you charge for your services, by the hour or day, flat fee, or as a markup on supplier costs, or a combination of both?
- What is your time worth?
- Will you charge for the proposal?
- What will the market bear?
- What about contingencies?
- What about taxes?

## ON WHAT BASIS, AND HOW MUCH, DO YOU CHARGE?

Most planners use either a straight markup of supplier costs or an hourly fee. In terms of a markup, standard practice seems to be in the 20 to 35% range. In answering this question, one must first consider the last question, what the market will bear. In some cases, it may be possible - and justifiable - to mark up at the higher end because the overall budget is higher and/or there is considerably more work involved than was anticipated. However, caution is advisable. If there is a competition, it may be worth decreasing your standard markup if the event is a large one, and taking a lower percentage. It is better to have a small part of **some** action than a large part of **no** action.

To determine what your time is worth in the simplest manner, calculate what your entire overhead is worth for the whole year, including your salary (or what you want to make!), and divide it by 235 (approx. average number of working days per year, allowing for 104 weekend days, 11 statutory holidays, and an average 15 working days vacation), then divide the result by 8 (number of working hours per day) to get the final answer. The formula looks like this:

$$\frac{\text{Total annual overhead (including planner's salary)}}{\text{235 (working days per year) x 8 (hours per working day)}} = \text{Hourly Fee (\$)}$$

Thus, if your total overhead is $24,000 (i.e. $2000 per month), and you want to make $50,000 per year, then you divide $74,000 by 1880 to arrive at an hourly fee of $39.36. This, of course, only ensures that you will break even if you work 100% of the time, so adding extra may be required.

How do you estimate the time it takes to plan an event? You can either charge a straight fee based on your best guess of the total time, or you can keep a running log of time spent, much like lawyers do. It is really up to you and your client as to what is the best arrangement.

Should you combine a markup with a fixed or hourly fee? This depends on what the work involves. Many planners do this. Our company sometimes does it to cover large events in which we also take responsibility for managing the distribution of all funds to suppliers and for contracting with them. In other words, we take the risk and do all the administration for supplier contracts. For this, we feel justified in charging an extra percentage on top of an hourly fee. However, this is typically very small in comparison to a straight supplier markup, more in the order of 10 to 15%.

## SHOULD YOU CHARGE FOR THE PROPOSAL?

Can you and should you charge for creating the proposal? Yes, if you think you can get away with it and the market will bear it. Once in a while, you may be able to do it, usually only if you agree to deduct the proposal fee from your overall fee if you land the account. Do keep in mind, though, that large creative proposals are time and labor-intensive and there is definitely justification for a charge if possible. An average of 28% of respondents in the 2003 Event Solutions survey charged for creative proposals.[3] It may also be a way - if you agree - for you to provide creative input for your client and not have them worry about intellectual property ownership if you are willing to give up that ownership for a fee.

## CONTINGENCIES

How do you handle contingencies? There are a couple of ways. First, if budget will allow, build in a contingency amount, and second, ensure contractually that you are covered in case of changes to client requirements or performer schedules. Ensure that all changes are made in writing and that you receive approval for the changes. There is more on this topic in the Contracts chapter.

## TAXES

How do you treat taxes? The only answer to that question is that it depends on the jurisdiction in which you work, specifically what country and what state or province. For example, in British Columbia, the event services industry is subject to a 6% federal goods and services tax on **all** event services. It is essentially what is known as a "flow-through" tax in which you must collect the tax based on the gross value of your services but you must also pay out based on the gross value of your suppliers' services. The difference in the two values is the amount that must be remitted to the federal government on a quarterly basis.

Provincial or state sales taxes are another matter and can get very complicated. There is very real potential for liability here and it behooves the event planner to understand the exact letter of the law and to get it in writing, specifically as it pertains to the event industry. In British Columbia, the law for the "social service tax," otherwise known as provincial sales tax, is extremely complicated. For example, an event planner is generally considered as an intermediate service provider and normally is not required to charge the provincial sales tax; however, the planner must **pay** the tax to suppliers and generally mark it up as part of the supplier cost. This represents a fundamental change to the way in which the tax used to be administered and, due to this regularly changing tax environment, the planner is strongly urged to always get in writing an exact interpretation of the law as it pertains to his particular business.

What about budgets for large public events? These are no different, just more complicated and complex than for smaller private events. The comments about markups and fees are still valid for these events. However, it is definitely necessary to keep a detailed spreadsheet for these complex events, usually divided into separate categories.

An example of each kind of event budget follows on the next three pages.

Table 7-1: Event Budget for a Small Private Event

| Item | Cost | | Retail Price with Markup | |
|---|---|---|---|---|
| **Entertainment** | | | | |
| Dance Band | $ | 3,000 | $ | 4,000 |
| 6 strolling look-alikes | $ | 1,800 | $ | 2,400 |
| Stage Show | | | | |
| - Dancers | $ | 1,200 | $ | 1,600 |
| - Magician | $ | 1,000 | $ | 1,330 |
| - MC | $ | 500 | $ | 670 |
| Total Entertainment | $ | 7,500 | $ | 10,000 |
| | | | | |
| **Décor** | | | | |
| 35 table centers | $ | 1,750 | $ | 2,340 |
| Stage backdrop | $ | 300 | $ | 400 |
| 35 table linens | $ | 700 | $ | 935 |
| 350 napkins | $ | 1,750 | $ | 2,335 |
| 350 chair covers | $ | 2,800 | $ | 3,740 |
| Total Décor | $ | 7,300 | $ | 9,750 |
| | | | | |
| **Production** | | | | |
| Room lighting and table pinspotting | $ | 5,000 | $ | 6,670 |
| Stage lighting | $ | 3,000 | $ | 4,000 |
| Audio | $ | 4,000 | $ | 5,335 |
| Stage management | $ | 300 | $ | 400 |
| Staging | $ | 2,000 | $ | 2,670 |
| Total Production | $ | 14,300 | $ | 19,070 |
| | | | | |
| **Total Event** | $ | 29,100 | $ | 38,820 |
| | | | | |
| **Gross Profit** | | | $ | 9720 |

Table 7-2: Event Budget for a Large Public Event

| Item | Amount |
|---|---:|
| **Revenue** | |
| Sponsorships | $ 150,000 |
| Ticket Sales (15,000 @ $20) | $ 300,000 |
| **Total Revenue** | **$ 450,000** |
| | |
| **Expenses** | |
| Marketing and public relations | |
| - Advertisements | $ 15,000 |
| - Mailouts | $ 20,000 |
| - VIP invitations and hosting | $ 10,000 |
| - Photography and video | $ 2,000 |
| - Program design and printing | $ 6,000 |
| - Ticket printing and sales commissions | $ 30,000 |
| Subtotal Marketing and PR | $ 83,000 |
| | |
| Talent | |
| - Headline Performers | $ 50,000 |
| - Accommodation for talent | $ 2,000 |
| - Backline equipment rental for band | $ 800 |
| - Transportation for talent | $ 3,000 |
| Subtotal Talent | $ 55,800 |
| | |
| Venue | |
| - Venue rental, including cleanup and ushering | $ 15,000 |
| - Security | $ 25,000 |
| - Signage | $ 2,500 |
| Subtotal Venue | $ 42,500 |
| | |
| Volunteers | |
| - T-Shirts | $ 2,000 |
| - Badging | $ 1,000 |
| - Food and beverage | $ 3,000 |
| Subtotal Volunteers | $ 6,000 |
| | |
| Administration | |
| - Staffing (3 @ $10,000) | $ 30,000 |

| | | |
|---|---|---|
| - Event Manager | $ | 20,000 |
| - Insurance | $ | 4,400 |
| - Contracting and office | $ | 2,300 |
| Subtotal Administration | $ | 56,700 |
| | | |
| Production | | |
| - Audio | $ | 12,000 |
| - Lighting | $ | 15,000 |
| - A-V | $ | 7,000 |
| - Staging and drape | $ | 6,500 |
| - Production manager and Tech Director | $ | 25,000 |
| - Stage managers (4 for 8 hours @ $25.00) | $ | 800 |
| Subtotal Production | $ | 66,300 |
| | | |
| **Total Expenses** | $ | 310,300 |
| | | |
| **Gross Profit** | $ | 139,700 |

# 8

# Ethical Considerations

## UNDERSTANDING THE ETHICS OF PROPOSALS

E thics is one of the current hot topics in the special events industry. It is not only hot, it is hotly debated, because whenever the topic arises, there are always people who do not see in black and white but in many shades of gray. There is the constant clash between what is morally and usually ethically right, and what is good for business. The current business climate requires one to do all that is possible to make money yet be ethically responsible at the same time. Generally speaking, if one approaches business with a moral and ethically responsible attitude, it is hard to go wrong, as this approach will yield more goodwill in the long term, even if it means missing some business in the short term. As this is a huge topic in the industry and it covers a multitude of scenarios, presented here will be some general guidelines pertaining primarily to proposals, and the issues surrounding copyright.

### Copyright and Intellectual Property

This is probably the most important concern for anyone, especially a planner, who is presenting original creative ideas. Ethically, the client is the one who has the responsibility to behave correctly, but in reality, it seldom happens. That means that you as the planner must protect your and your suppliers' creative ideas and rights.

To begin with - and legally - it is generally agreed that the "idea" belongs to the person who actually writes and describes the creative concept. Therefore, if you are the one who describes in detail how your event will flow and how the décor will look, then you are the creator and the "owner" of the concept. If your decorator designs and describes the room décor and all the unbelievably new and wonderful table dressings, then it is she who owns the idea. Note that this ownership continues on past the original description and presentation, which means that theoretically, any designs you see in a magazine cannot be used by anyone except the original owner unless that person authorizes its use. This, of course, also applies to you and your suppliers.

How do you protect your ownership? There are two main ways to at least help you:

- Payment. Again, the concept of payment for creative work enters the picture. If you are preparing an extensive proposal, you can ask for a fee and then tell clients that they are free to use the ideas provided you are paid for the creation of them (not recommended because they can then get anyone to do the work and you no longer have any rights to the ideas).
- Copyright statement. This basically acts as a deterrent to clients who may wish to gather your ideas and then use them themselves or get another planner or company to do the work. A sample statement that we use, in BOLD, large font type on a single page either at the end or the beginning of a proposal is the following.

**"PLEASE NOTE THAT THE FOREGOING PROPOSAL AND ALL INFORMATION IT CONTAINS IS THE CONFIDENTIAL AND PROPRIETARY INTELLECTUAL PROPERTY OF ABC EVENT COMPANY LTD. ALL RIGHTS ARE RESERVED AND NO PART OF THE PROPOSAL OR THE INFORMATION IT CONTAINS MAY BE REPRODUCED, COPIED, USED OR MODIFIED IN ANY WAY WITHOUT THE EXPRESS PRIOR WRITTEN PERMISSION OF ABC EVENT COMPANY LTD.**

**THIS INCLUDES, WITHOUT LIMITATION, THE USE AND/OR MODIFICATION OF ANY CONCEPTS OR IDEAS PERTAINING TO ENTERTAINMENT, DÉCOR OR THE PRODUCTION OF THIS EVENT. INCLUDED IN THIS RESTRICTION IS THE USE AND/OR BOOKING OF ANY OF THE ENTERTAINMENT (ACTS OR PERFORMERS) RECOMMENDED BY ABC EVENT COMPANY LTD. FOR THIS PARTICULAR EVENT IF IT IS PRODUCED BY ANY COMPANY OR ORGANIZATION OTHER THAN ABC EVENT COMPANY LTD.**

**ANY BREACH OF THIS RESTRICTION WILL RESULT IN LEGAL ACTION BEING TAKEN TO RECOVER, WITHOUT LIMITATION, ALL COSTS ASSOCIATED WITH THE CREATION OF THIS PROPOSAL AND ALL PROFITS THAT WOULD HAVE COME TO ABC EVENT COMPANY LTD. IF ABC EVENT COMPANY LTD. HAD PRODUCED THIS EVENT.**

**© 2003 ABC EVENT COMPANY LTD.**

Note that this statement may not be enforceable in its entirety in a court of law, but at the very least, it is a strong deterrent to potential copyright thieves. We lovingly refer to it as our CYA ("cover your ass") statement!

## Using Other People's Ideas for Your Proposal

When considering using other people's ideas for your proposal, all the same criteria apply to you as above. You cannot simply view an idea in a magazine and take it as your own, although many people do. Ethically - and arguably legally - it is wrong. The best alternative is to acknowledge it as the other person's work and if the client likes it, state that you will attempt to get approval to use the concepts. Usually, if the work has been published, the designer will probably allow it or at least part of it. If there is a special creation like a costume, he might insist that you use the original.

## Other Ethics Issues

There are several other issues that regularly come up pertaining to ethics in the industry and some general guidelines will be given:

- Obtaining supplier contacts. No, it is not all right to solicit a supplier's contact information if that supplier is working for another person or company. A case in point might be a band you see at a competitor's event. It is definitely not ethically correct to solicit the phone number of the band directly from them. Always think what it would be like if the shoe were on the other foot.

- Bidding against yourself. Often, some planners are requested to submit a quote for the same event by more than one person/company. It is ethically irresponsible to submit a proposal without notifying and obtaining the permission of both potential clients. A good guideline is to tell the second requestor that you have been asked by the first and will check to see if it is OK, especially if it is exactly the same proposal. It is usually better to offer to submit a **different** proposal only if the first requestor agrees to it. At least this constant flow of information ensures that everyone knows that you are ethical. Don't be afraid to lose business in these cases, as they are ones that truly test and prove your ethics. This responsible ethical attitude will serve you well in the future.

# Part Four

# Resources

# 9

## What Exactly are Resources?

Resources are, simply put, the essential elements of the event itself. Most often they are the tried, trusted, and true suppliers that you as the event planner must depend on to deliver your event and to meet the expectations of the client. Even the most creative and skilled planner is useless without a significant library or database of resources into which she can weave the creative ideas. How does one acquire such a database and in turn, readily access it when required? There are three ways:

### CONTINUE TO LEARN

Make it a point to attend at least two or three continuing education courses and at least one conference per year in the field of special events. Make sure that you attend a conference that has a trade show component that enables you to see and try out the latest inventions in the business, and to talk to suppliers directly. Some examples include the Canadian Special Events and Meetings Exhibition, the Special Event (put on by Special Events Magazine), and the Event Solutions Expo (put on by Event Solutions Magazine).

### STAY CURIOUS

Don't pass up any opportunity to gain new insights and ideas. Always be on the lookout for new concepts, décor, entertainment, and innovative ways to use simple items. Some examples of sources of ideas include:

- Toy stores or most any store
- Magazines
- Newspapers
- TV

- Internet
- Restaurants
- Theme parks.

## KEEP DETAILED RECORDS

This will entail gathering contact information (names, phone and fax numbers, e-mail addresses, web site addresses, physical addresses) and keeping notes about new ideas, including pictures, promotional material, and costs. Keep it all on a good data base and categorize the information by type of supplier so that it is easily retrievable when needed.

There are endless resources out there and we will deal only with the main ones that get the most use at special events. This book is intended as a practical guide and therefore we will go into some detail about each of the resources so that the planner will have a better understanding of what they are all about, what the current state of the art is in each one, and how they might be used in the creative process to come up with a winning idea for the event.

# 10

# Entertainment

Entertainment is the one thing people remember long after an event is over. Why? Because entertainment touches something deep within us. It invokes strong feelings, emotions, and memories, and it affects many of our senses. The more of these feelings, emotions, memories and senses you can affect, the more successful will be your presentation.

## TYPES OF ENTERTAINMENT

There are several categories of live entertainment, the main ones being:

- Name acts or celebrity talent. These include nationally and internationally known performers.
- Musical variety. These include comedy music, background music (mainly instrumentalists), soloists, symphony orchestras, and marching bands.
- Dance bands. These can be everything from duos to orchestras.
- Variety. These are the unusual types of entertainers including jugglers, magicians, ventriloquists, clowns, hypnotists, and such.
- Ethnic or cultural. Native Indian, Asian, Latin, and all other cultural performances that stress heritage.
- Interactive. This can be anything in which the main goal is for people to participate such as virtual reality games, table acts, and strolling acts who interact with people.
- There are definitely other types of entertainment such as A-V and special effects, but we deal here with strictly live entertainment.

# USES OF ENTERTAINMENT

This is where your real knowledge of resources and creativity enter the picture. You will need to know that there are many ways to use entertainment that are unconventional. The important thing to remember here is that this can form the basis for convincing your client of the ROI (return on investment) to be gained by using your entertainment ideas. Here are the main uses:

## Education

You can subtly impart some knowledge to the audience; it can be all based on learning or can be a small part of a show. For example, we once used an improvisational (improv) comedy troupe to act out scenarios as a learning tool for financial planners and psychologists.

## Physically Move

Make the audience go where you want. Sometimes using a marching band or other "noisy" entertainment to lead people can save considerable time, especially with a large group.

## Emotionally Move

Anytime you can stir an audience inside, they will be at your mercy and you can impart almost any message you want to them. Basically, this is done through the choice of material presented (e.g. patriotic songs, sad or memory-invoking songs).

## Motivate

Typically used to "pump up" a sales force, this can be everything from motivational speakers to cheerleaders to high energy dancers.

## Decoration

Costumed living statues, interactive entertainers, look-alikes, and even costumed guests can often be a very cost-effective use of entertainment.

## Announce

Special announcements can be made with MCs, herald trumpets, personalized video greetings from automated talking heads, strolling "robots" at a trade show, and similar concepts.

## Introduce

Novel ways to launch a product can be done with entertainment. Typical examples include a magical "reveal" created by a magician, fireworks, and even "off-the-wall" stuff. We once introduced a new Vancouver to Boston airline service by photographing a Paul Revere character riding a horse in front of a taxiing 747 while holding a huge banner announcing the service!

## Advertise

Advertising products can easily be done through entertainment. One of our clients (a gas company) made the front page of the local newspaper when we dressed up two actors as a new baby and Father Time and had them lighting a giant 15 ft tall gas torch like an Olympic flame, just before New Year's.

## Create Ambience

Creating an atmosphere for easy discussion, for conducting business (very important), and for relaxing is one of the most popular uses of entertainment. This can be as simple as a background music group conducive to conducting easy discussions and making business deals or as crazy as a beach band entering the party in a "Woodie" complete with surf boards and girls in bikinis.

## Enjoyment

Sometimes entertainment has no other purpose than pure enjoyment, but usually there is some ulterior motive, such as an award for top sales people (e.g. an incentive event).

# PRESENTATION OF ENTERTAINMENT

Now that we have discussed the types and uses of entertainment, there are some critical areas to be addressed in determining how to actually present it. The following are some important considerations:

- Understand the purpose or goal of the client and even your own goal in using this particular form of entertainment. It will help you to determine the best way to present it.
- Strive for the unusual. This applies to the actual performance and to the type of performers; consider outlandish costumes and unusual combinations of performers.
- Try to involve as much of the audience as possible in the entertainment. If the venue is large, try to find a way to let the back half of the audience see some entertainment, such as having performers enter from the back or sides of a room instead of from backstage, or by using satellite stages. In this way, the entire audience feels that they have been given better value for their money.

- Often several lesser-known performers are better than one big name act. Two reasons for this are that one big name act can be very costly and also that there is a better chance of the entire audience enjoying several acts than all of them enjoying just one act for which a lot of money has been paid.

- Look for three main factors in booking entertainers that will usually guarantee success: absolute perfection at their craft, whether they are singers, jugglers or any other type; some inclusion of a comedic element in their act; and some form of audience involvement.

- Try to keep shows to a maximum of 50-60 minutes in length to alleviate boredom, which can occur no matter who is performing, where it is, or who the audience is. The old adage about leaving them wanting more is still true.

- Strive for emotional impact through selective choice of performance material.

- Timing is everything. The ideal show is totally seamless no matter what is happening on stage, or how many different stage changeovers there are. Plan ahead and ensure everyone is in the right place well ahead of time.

- Treat your entertainers well and keep them informed with up-to-the minute information about who they are performing for and what is expected of them. Also, try to give them a changing area (also known as a "green room") that is quiet and clean. Just like anyone else, if they are made to feel special, they will enjoy doing their job more and that will come across to the audience.

- Don't spoil the show by scrimping on production (sound and lights). If you are spending good money on an entertainer, it is not worth ruining the show by having an inferior sound system or inadequate lighting.

- Know your audience demographics ahead of time **before** you book any entertainment so you can match the entertainment to what is most suitable for them. For example, having a comedian for a group of Japanese businessmen who may only understand 25% of the show will spell disaster, as will a loud rock band for a group of 50-60 year-olds.

- If at all possible, use the services of an entertainment agency or production company well versed in the needs and idiosyncrasies of the type of event you are planning. For example, an agency which normally books night club acts will not be as good at booking acts for the corporate market and will probably not have as suitable a roster of talent. Most definitely, an agency or production company should be able to make your life a lot easier by offering a greater selection of talent, by doing all the negotiating and contracting for you, and by being there to ensure nothing goes wrong.

# 11

# Décor

Special event décor is a moving target. There are so many new items coming on the market on a regular basis and so many new themes that are popular each year that it is almost impossible for a new planner to keep track. However, there are some essentials that one needs to know.

## TYPES OF DÉCOR

Décor can be broken down into several general categories and most falls into at least one of these:

### Backdrops and Sets

These include large painted murals, generally made of canvas or treated synthetic material, large theatrical-type sets (e.g. old town sets, 50s diners, etc), and hardwall stage sets.

### Costumes

Large, elaborate costumes are becoming more and more popular and are so outrageous that they can now fit into the category of décor.

### Fabrics

These include all linens (mostly for tables), chair covers, draperies, banners, spandex sculptures, and other soft goods.

### Florals

Although seemingly obvious, these can also include large temporary "environments" such as jungles and silk flowers, plus live trees.

## Inflatables

These include ordinary balloons both helium and air-filled, large advertising-type inflatables, air tubes, wind tubes, and similar new inventions.

## Props

This includes most other décor not in the above categories, including small props used for displays and table centers, ice bars and ice carvings, lighting fixtures used for décor (e.g. small table lamps or battery-powered mini-lights), foam board sculptures, and much more.

## Technical Décor

This category would include such new technologies as tabletop, closed circuit, battery-powered TV monitors, lighting (gobos and intelligent lights, to be covered later) and A-V (large screen presentations and projections on buildings and soft goods).

# USING DÉCOR

Because of the differing opinions and wide variety of options available, this can be an extensive subject. There are some general guidelines in the use of décor:

- Watch **all** dimensions in a room. If budget permits, try to make the room look full in every direction. For example, even if there are no wall decorations, tall centerpieces can make a room look very full just by themselves. Likewise, items hung from the ceiling tend to de-emphasize the room's height and help to make the space more intimate.
- Match the scale of the décor to the scale of the room. Very large props in a small room are just as ridiculous as very small props in a large room. In a medium-sized room, generally speaking, large props are the most impressive and have the most impact.
- Try for color coordination in all décor, including table linens, napkins, centerpieces, walls, ceiling treatment, carpet, and right down even to the gaff tape used to tape down electrical cords.
- Try for texture variation to increase the effects on different senses (e.g. touch) as a highly sensual experience is more memorable.
- Allow sufficient time for all setup. This may seem self-evident but there are always delays for something, so add one or two extra staff over the amount calculated and allow for 1.5 times the setup time calculated to account for these delays (e.g. anything from

slow freight elevator access to dining tables being rearranged at the last minute).

- If on a limited budget, concentrate décor in the main focal points of the room, specifically the entrances, tables, room corners, and stage if there is one.

- Soft décor (e.g. fabrics, canvas backdrop, and florals) is generally easier to work with than hard décor (e.g. flats and large solid props). It is also easier to transport and quite often cheaper, plus it tends to more easily and cost effectively cover larger areas.

- Don't forget to light your décor. Many great events have been only mediocre because there was insufficient lighting to highlight the beautiful décor. If possible, use a professional lighting designer who is familiar with lighting special events.

- When using props, strive for realism. For example, if creating a western set, don't use fake wagon wheels leaning up against a fake corral fence. Use the real thing. Your audience will love it.

- Use people as décor. Costumed actors and models wandering about the event can be even more effective than static décor and are virtually a necessity for many themes these days.

- Use professional decorators who are familiar with the special event industry. It will be well worth it in the end. These people know where to find exactly the right décor that will fit your budget and will save you much time and grief.

# 12

# Lighting

This is one of the fastest growing technical fields in special events. Used for meetings, rock and roll concerts, outdoor architectural highlights, and every type of special event, lighting can be costly, frustrating, and power-hungry and yet still provide a truly awesome component to your event. It is certainly one of the primary ways to achieve emotional impact. Here is a very basic initiation into this fascinating field, courtesy of Steve Matthews of Show Time Lighting[4], along with some personal experience also incorporated.

Often neglected, especially in meeting planning, lighting plays a major, although somewhat subtle, role in event planning. Good design should enhance the overall effect and event experience without drawing too much attention to itself as a separate entity. How is this accomplished? Mainly by attention to the conceptual and physical design details. The main considerations in lighting design include:

## CONCEPTUAL DESIGN

What is being lit and what concept does the client or planner have in mind? Does the planner want to create only ambience or actually light something specific? Here are the components of conceptual design:

### Theme

This refers to the enhancement of a specific event theme through the use of lighting, and can vary from complementing a theme's colors to lighting props, tables, walls, floors, and ceiling.

### Ambience

What type of event is this? If it is a rock concert, or dinner and dance for a 20-something crowd, lighting will be vastly different from that to be used at an awards dinner for senior business people.

## Practical Illumination

This refers to more of the plain, less creative use of lighting for such mundane items as stage backdrops, lecterns, image magnification (IMAG) and video, and guest speakers.

These questions must be asked and the answers understood before the lighting designer can begin the design. Once the answers are known, then the designer moves on to the practical application of lighting.

# PRACTICAL DESIGN

There are some key basics to lighting for all the above concepts that will help the event planner to understand the process of design and how to make it work better:

## Lighting for Themes and Décor

Décor and event theming using light is a vast field with perhaps only a handful of truly gifted lighting designers in North America. When it is done well, it is usually the single event component that causes gasps from guests as they enter the event space. Some of the considerations include:

- Use complimentary colors for props such as greens to enhance trees and reds or ambers to enhance wood.
- Choose the event colors at the outset with the event designer and try to keep the lighting in those color families.
- Use lighting in conjunction with special effects, each to enhance the other. Examples include lighting along a path at floor level under fog, wild intelligent light movement to enhance indoor pyro or confetti cannons, or lighting effects and gobo patterns on a water scrim.
- Don't forget all the dimensions and all the possible surfaces within the event space. They can all be used for lighting: ceilings for cloud patterns or changing colors; walls for theme gobos or uplighting; and floors for gobos, color washes, and wild movement.
- Strive for the unusual, such as: lighting under tables; unique lighting of table centers (not necessarily pin spots but battery powered electrical colored wiring or mini lights); reverse lighting of the audience instead of the event space and walls; and lighting of different event elements and theme prop vignettes at different times as the

event progresses.

- Fly instruments as much as possible in order to minimize clutter and distraction. For example, pinspotting table centers from above is extremely effective and classy.
- Keep instruments hidden from view and out of people's eyes.

## Lighting for Ambience

If this can be done very subtly, the effect is better and often can affect the "mood" of the event and of the guests. Some considerations are:

- Use indirect lighting for such things as walls and ceilings, pillars, and tables.
- Use colors that are mood-enhancing and that reflect the theme.
- Try using color-changing instruments that can be programmed to change slowly over time and thus give a continuously "new" look and feel to the event every few minutes.

## Lighting for Practical Purposes

Most events have some element of the more mundane such as the need to light the company president giving his annual address or the award recipients as they come onstage. This type of lighting also has its own set of considerations:

- Lighting for live entertainment. Use front lighting to illuminate performers for visibility, but back lighting to create energy and to set the mood for the performance. The inclusion of moving lights on a back line is common in many high-energy performances.
- Lighting for the camera (still or video). Use of colored filters is not recommended as the cameras require common light color among all fixtures as well as a consistent temperature. Cameras are less forgiving of color variations than is the human eye. Backlight is also essential to create a visual separation between the subject and the background.
- Lighting people. Front light should come from two sides to eliminate shadow. Use complimentary colored filters to enhance the appearance of good health. Generally, warm colors (pinks and ambers) improve the apparent health of the subject and cool colors (blues and lavenders) enhance the colors in clothing and sets. Backlighting is recommended, although not always necessary, again to separate the subject from the background.

### Lighting for Attention

This refers to the "flash" effects and newer concepts:

- Logo projection using a gobo design is simple, inexpensive, and rewarding. Everyone likes to see their name in lights, and they can be projected on walls, ceilings, floors, and screens.
- Automated or intelligent lighting is an excellent way to add professional pizzazz and high-energy "flash" to an awards show or gala event.

# PHYSICAL DESIGN

The physical design of the event lighting refers to "how" it will be accomplished. This is when the designer brings out his "toolbox" and puts the right instruments in the right number in the right location and makes the magic happen. Some considerations include:

### Venue Physical Characteristics

The lighting designer needs to know:

- Shape of the room. Is it open, square, or full of columns? All of these will have an effect on the types and quantity of lights used.
- Ceiling height and design. If the ceiling is too high or too low, lighting will be impacted and the effects either heightened or lessened, requiring either more or fewer instruments. If large chandeliers or complex recesses form large parts of the ceiling, extra lights may be needed or a different approach taken. For example, lighting can be reflected off large crystal chandeliers without the chandeliers being turned on, to create spectacular colored ambient effects on the ceiling.
- Control of existing house and ambient lighting. Will daylight through windows or translucent ceiling material such as tenting be a factor in lighting design? Where and how is house lighting controlled and can a remote controller be used at a lighting control console in order to save time and effort in turning house lights on and off?

### Type and Location of Lighting Support

Should lighting be flown (rigged from the ceiling) or ground supported on stands? If flown, the designer must know the exact location of ceiling hanging points, how many there are, and what their load rating is. Keep in mind that flying lighting or audio is normally a much more expensive proposition than ground supporting it due to the additional work required, sometimes including the use of qualified union labor, extra time to rig the ceiling points, and time delay for other installation components such as décor and dining tables.

If stands are used, prime locations must be chosen to permit optimum lighting of stages and sets without blocking sight lines, without creating hazards to foot traffic, by eliminating lights in guests' eyes, and by minimizing cable runs. If there are pillars in the room or sets and other décor elements that might block the path of light from any instruments, then the design must be changed or a new support method devised. Finally, if followspots are to be used, where is the optimum location for them and will risers be required to elevate them to the required height?

## Types of Instruments

Deciding on the number and type of lights to use is what makes a good designer and can make or break the effectiveness of the lighting design. Of all the instruments available from his toolbox, the designer must choose the ones that will work the best for your goals and your event, including your budget. In making this decision, the lighting designer must consider:

- Required intensity. How bright must each element of lighting be to give the effect desired? Most lights come in multiples of 100 watts power, which is another measure of intensity.
- Required color. What is being lit and how will it be affected by different colors? Are colors required to enhance the effect? What gels or gobos to use will be determined after considering color.
- Required coverage. How big an area must each light cover? Do you only have the budget for eight lights to illuminate a 32 ft wide and 24 ft deep stage or can more lights be added? The answer will determine the number and type of light to be used.
- Required functionality. Is some high-energy pizzazz needed or just static lighting for a speech? Will the person or thing being lit be in motion? The more pizzazz, the more costly because intelligent lights will probably be used.
- What will the total power consumption be? See below for more details on this subject.
- What is the budget for lighting?

Table 12-1 gives the definitions of some of the more common types of lighting instruments and what they are used for.

# LIGHTING CONTROL

Where will it be and will technicians be required to operate the lights during the event? Usually, the best location for controlling lighting is directly in the middle at the back of the event space; however, reality does not always allow this. The designer must know the exact location in relation to power supplied in order to determine the length and routing of cable runs. In addition, the designer must know if he will be in a position to easily view the lit objects or people, if there will be a raised platform for the control and if a remote house light control will be available.

# POWER FOR LIGHTING

Electrical power is possibly the single most important consideration for ensuring that the lights will actually work - and keep working - during an event. There is nothing more embarrassing than having an electrical circuit breaker blow during the president's keynote address or the finale of a rock concert by a name act. The culprit in these cases is almost always the power being drawn by lighting. Knowing the power requirements of a given event lighting design ahead of time is essential to avoid this type of embarrassing moment.

If the lighting designer knows his stuff, he will have calculated the exact power draw of his design and will convey to you the event planner, exactly what he needs from the venue - or from an external, portable power source if outdoors or in a location where no existing power is available. Armed with this knowledge, you can then liaise with the venue and request the power drop required. You will also need to know - or ask - if the venue allows for the lighting company to install their own connection (may be possible if one of the lighting staff is a qualified, licensed electrician) or if you or the client will have to pay for a house electrician to be called in to install the connection. You will also have to specify exactly when and where the power drop is needed so that it is available when the lighting team arrives for setup.

## Determining Power Requirements for Lighting

Lighting uses the basic formula that you probably learned in high school but have long since forgotten:

$$P = I \times V$$

Here, P is power in watts, I is current draw in amps, and V is voltage in volts.

The power is expressed as watts (W) or kilowatts (KW, equivalent to 1000 W). Each lighting fixture has a power and that is usually proportional to the amount (intensity) of light that it throws. Most modern stage lights are notorious power hogs, drawing from 100 to 1000 W each. To determine total power, work with your lighting designer and add up all the lights' total wattage. For example, eight Par 64 stage lights each drawing 1000 W will require 8000 W of power.

Using the formula above, if the voltage of the standard circuit is 120 V and the amperage of the standard circuit is 15 amps, then the total power available from a single venue wall power outlet is 1800 W, far short of the power needed for your stage lights. You will need to either use eight separate 120 V circuits (a very risky proposition in a venue!) or opt for tying into a higher power source of 208 V. This power can come in up to 3 phases and offers much more total power because it can also provide higher amperage.

Generally - and not considering a slightly more correct but very theoretical approach - using the following guidelines can help you determine your total power requirements and the associated costs, since the more power that is used, the higher the cost:

- Less than 1500 W draw. Use one, preferably two, 120 V outlets.
- Less than about 10,000 W draw. Use a 208 V, 50 amp tie-in.
- Between 10,000 W and 30,000 W. Use a 208 V, 100 amp, three-phase tie-in, which gives three of what are called "legs," each with 120 V and 100 amps.
- Greater than 30,000 W. You begin to get into major concert-type lighting and will need 208 V, 200 amp, three-phase power or more.

You will definitely need professional lighting help and a qualified electrician's assistance as you get into the more elaborate setups.

## SCHEDULING AND OTHER CONSIDERATIONS

Lighting often requires more time for setup due to the complex nature of the lighting itself, and the fact that ceiling rigging may take a long time and may only be able to be accomplished at times when nobody else is working, such as between midnight and 6:00am. For these reasons, and to determine staff numbers, the lighting designer will need to know:

- How early they can get in for setup, possibly up to 48 hours before the event
- How long it will take to move their equipment into the venue and room
- Who will be competing for floor space
- Whether special lighting will be needed
- Whether "dark time" for programming (note that most intelligent lights need to be pre-programmed to be most effective) and focus will be needed
- How long the show is
- What time "strike" will begin
- What time strike must be complete
- If there will be competition for floor space during strike
- If the event will require a lighting operator
- Accessibility for truck at the loading dock and availability of truck parking
- If the venue is union run and if specialized workers such as riggers are required
- If any special permits or badging will be required.

Table 12-1: Glossary of Lighting Terminology and Description of Equipment

| Term | Description |
|------|-------------|
| **Accent Light** | 1. Illumination used to make something stand out. It may be done with intensity and/or color.<br>2. A luminaire that provides such illumination. |
| **Aircraft Landing Light (ACL)** | A high intensity, tight beam Par lamp that derives its name from its use as an aircraft landing lamp. The true ACL is 28 V and 250 W, although there are many variations. Often used to add dramatic effect to stage shows. |
| **Automated Lights** (also known as **Intelligent Lights** or **Moving Lights**) | These come in several types, primarily moving yolk (or moving head) and moving mirror fixtures. In yolk fixtures, the whole instrument (light) can pan and tilt (i.e. move in the X and Y axes). In mirror fixtures, only a small mirror moves to send the beam off in other directions. |
| **Automated Fixture Control Console** | A lighting control console designed specifically for the purpose of controlling and storing/playing back cues for automated fixtures. These consoles often have subsystems for controlling different features of automated fixtures such as color change, gobo, and focus position. Complex cue structures, effects, and chases are typical features of automated fixture control consoles. Three primary types of automated fixture consoles include: proprietary consoles designed to work primarily with one type or brand of automated fixture; generic controllers which are programmed to control many different types of automated fixtures; and hybrid controllers which combine the functions of standard theatrical memory consoles with those of an automated fixture console. |
| **Back Light** | A lighting design term referring to any light that comes primarily from behind the actor, musician, or object being lit. Backlighting is associated with strong highlights or halo effects. |
| **Baffle** | A sheet of material used to prevent a spill of light in a lantern or in part of a set. |

| | |
|---|---|
| **Ballyhoo** | Followspot move in which the operator continuously moves the beam in a figure-eight motion around the stage or audience. This term is also used to describe similar movements performed by moving lights. |
| **Bare-Ends** | An electrical term referring to the ends of a feeder cable set which do not have any permanent connector attached to them. Bare ends are often used to tie dimmer feeder cable into a house power supply or company switch. |
| **Barndoors** | A rotatable attachment consisting of two or four metal flaps (hinged) which are fixed to the front of a Fresnel or plano-convex type lantern to cut off the beam in a particular direction. |
| **Batten** | A horizontal pipe on which luminaires, scenery, curtains, and some distribution equipment are hung. |
| **Batten Strip** | A connector strip hung from a batten. |
| **Beam** | 1. Generally, the conoid, or in some cases, the pyramoid of light emanating from a luminaire. |
| | 2. In photometry, the circular area of the base of a cone-shaped beam where the intensity is at least 50% of the maximum intensity. The maximum intensity is ideally located at the center of the base. It should be noted that some luminaires, such as ellipsoidal spotlights and followspots, can be adjusted or designed such that the light emanating from them does not include the entire beam, (i.e. the edge of the beam is greater than 50% of its center). |
| **Beam Angle** | The angle of the cone of light produced by a light. |
| **Beam Pattern** | The complete shape of the beam, as defined in the general sense. It includes any realistic or abstract patterns introduced into the beam as well as any apparatus that alters the contour of the beam. |
| **Blacklight** | An ultraviolet (UV) light source used to create special lighting effects with fluorescent materials. UV sources can be incandescent, fluorescent, or preferably HID lamps. |

| | |
|---|---|
| **Blackout** | A lighting design term referring to a light cue that takes the stage quickly into darkness. A blackout is often abbreviated B/O. |
| **Blinders** | Lamps arranged around the stage directed into the auditorium, used mainly for effect in rock concerts and other events. |
| **Board** | The main control for the stage lighting. |
| **Border** | A narrow horizontal masking piece (usually cloth), normally of neutral color (black) to mask the flown lighting rig from the audience. |
| **Bounce** | Diffuse light that has been reflected from the stage, walls, cyclorama, etc. |
| **Box Truss** | An aluminum or steel support structure often used for temporary rigging of lights, scenery, or sound equipment. As the name suggests, a box truss is rectangular in shape creating a rigid structure which is easy to stack and load onto a truck. An additional advantage of box truss over other truss shapes is the ability to hang lighting instruments inside the truss, where they can remain protected while in transport. |
| **Break-Out** | A cable-connecting device that breaks a multi-circuit cable (multi- cable) into individual circuits. |
| **Break-up** | A commonly used abstract gobo that gives a textured effect to the light, without throwing a specific pattern onto the stage. Used to add interest to light beams. A leafy breakup is used for outdoor scenes/forests/spooky wood etc. to break up the light. |
| **Bridle** | A rigging device or method that distributes a single point of a load to more than one hanging point. |
| **Bump Button** | A momentary switch or button on a lighting control console that brings a channel to a level of full when pressed. Bump buttons allow rapid manual control over lighting control channels. On some consoles bump buttons can be put into solo mode where all channels except those controlled by the bump button go out. |

| | |
|---|---|
| **Bump Cue** | A lighting cue that happens instantly. Bump cues are traditionally used to emphasize similar abrupt changes in music, choreography, or to mark the end of a scene. A bump cue where all lights go out is called a blackout. |
| **Cable** | Common term describing any number of types of electrical connecting devices. All cables employ some type of conductor, usually stranded copper wire, and some type of insulation to protect it. Common cable types related to stage lighting include: stage cable, multi-cable, feeder cable, and control cable. |
| **Cable Bundle** | A group of electrical cables attached at various points by tape, rope, etc. |
| **Cable Cradle** | A metal sling used to support heavy stage cable as it hangs from a batten, while simultaneously preventing the cable from entering horizontal sight lines from the house to the stage. It can also take strain away from the point where the cable exits a piece of distribution equipment. |
| **Cable Drop** | An overhead electric cable or group of electric cables that extends downward for the connection of luminaires or other electrical apparatuses. The cable(s) may be connected to some type of overhead support, or directly to a piece of distribution equipment. |
| **Cable Tie** | Lockable (and sometimes releasable) plastic strap used to tie a bundle of cables together. |
| **Camlock (TM)** | A locking single contact connector commonly used to connect feeder cables and portable dimmer racks. |
| **Chain Hoist** | A lifting device comprised of an electric motor and gear/chain drive system. Chain hoists are commonly used to lift portable trusses into place in order to "fly" lights for shows. |
| **Channel or Control Channel** | A complete control path for signals in lighting or sound equipment. On manual or preset controllers this may refer to an actual fader or slider. On a computer memory console, a channel may only be represented by a number that is assigned by the system to control any number of physical dimmers, color scrollers, or other devices. |

| | |
|---|---|
| **Chase** | A repeated sequence of changing lighting states. A chase can be as simple as a single string of lights flashed sequentially around a sign by a mechanical or electronic switching device (chaser or chase unit). By utilizing the chase (or effect) functions of a computer memory console, a chase can also comprise complex multi-part cues affecting large groups of lighting instruments. |
| **Choppers** | Two horizontal masking shutters used in followspots to shape the beam above and below. |
| **Color Boomerang** | A levered frame device within a followspot which allows different color filters to be introduced into the beam. Standard followspot boomerangs have space for six or seven different colors to be inserted. During a show individual or combined frames can be quickly added or dropped from the beam as needed. |
| **Color Changer** | 1. Scroller. A long string of up to 16 colors is passed horizontally in front of a lamp. Remotely controlled by the lighting desk. |
| | 2. Wheel. Electrically or manually operated disc which is fitted to the front of a lamp with several apertures holding different color filters which can be selected to enable color changes. Can also be selected to run continuously. |
| **Color Filter** | Color media placed in front of or within a lighting fixture to alter the color of the light produced. Filters for conventional fixtures are often made of a dyed polyester film. Since dyed filters work by absorbing unwanted colors and passing desired colors, they deteriorate from heat and must be replaced when they "burn up." Automated fixtures use more permanent dichroic color filters that are created by vacuum depositing thin films onto heat resistant glass. |
| **Color Mixing** | Combining the effects of two or more lighting gels: |
| | 1. Additive. Focusing two differently colored beams of light onto the same area (e.g. cyc floods). Combining colors in this way adds the colors together, eventually |

arriving at white. The three primary colors additively mix to form white, as do the complementary colors.

2. Subtractive. Placing two different gels in front of the same lantern. Subtractive mixing is used to obtain a color effect that is not available from stock or from manufacturers. Because the ranges of color are so wide, the need for subtractive mixing is reducing. Combining colors in this way reduces the light towards blackness. The three primary colors mix subtractively to form black (or to block all the light).

| | |
|---|---|
| **Color Rendering Index (CRI)** | A single number approximate evaluation of the effect of a light source on the visual appearance of a colored surface. The number falls on a scale from below 0 to 100, with daylight at 100. Objects and people viewed under lamps with a high CRI generally appear more true to life. |
| **Color Temperature** | The measurement of the color quality ("warmth" or "coolness") of a lamp measured in degrees Kelvin. A standard 1000 W tungsten halogen theatrical lamp has a color temperature of around 3200 Kelvin (K). |
| **Complementary Colors** | Two colors of light that combine to make white light in the additive color mixing system. For red, green, and blue, the complementary colors are cyan, magenta, and yellow, respectively. |
| **Computer Memory Console** | A lighting console in which cues can be stored and executed electronically. Computer consoles also employ many show editing and cue building functions that make the cue writing or programming process easier. Computer consoles can be divided into three basic types: cue-only type consoles, theatrical "classic" tracking consoles, and automated fixture control consoles. |
| **Cool Color** | Generally, a color that is in the green-blue-violet range. |
| **Cool Light** | Light having a color temperature of approximately 3600° K to 4900° K, (i.e. bright-white to blue-white). |

| | |
|---|---|
| **Controller** | A lighting control console or light board. Common types include the preset board, the computer memory console, as well as specialized automated fixture controllers such as the Vari-Lite Artisan II console. |
| **Conventional Lighting Fixture** | A standard lighting fixture such as a PAR can, Fresnel, or ERS, which offers no built-in automated functions. |
| **Cracked Oil Fog Machine** | A simple type of fog machine that atomizes oil into a fine atmosphere, usually by introducing compressed air into a reservoir containing mineral oil. Crackers are also available which crack water into a very fine mist. Haze machines produce effects similar to oil crackers without leaving an oily residue on surfaces. It has been found to be carcinogenic. |
| **Cross Bar** | 1. In the theater industry, a bar mounted horizontally on top of a stand. It contains two or more sliding tees for mounting luminaires, and a fixed tee for mounting the bar to the stand.<br>2. In the film and video industries, a bar mounted horizontally between two stands for the purpose of hanging luminaires or grip equipment. |
| **Cross Fade** | A lighting design term referring to a cue in which one set of lights increases in intensity while another set simultaneously decreases in intensity. |
| **Cue Light** | A light used to signal a cue. Red usually means stand by and green usually means execute the cue. |
| **Cyberlight (TM)** | Originally introduced in 1993, the Cyberlight is a moving mirror type automated fixture manufactured by Lightwave Research/High End Systems. |
| **Cyclorama (Cyc)** | A vertical surface which is used to form the background for a theatrical-type setting, usually made of heavy cloth drawn tight to achieve a smooth, flat surface. It usually represents the sky or suggests limitless space. Traditionally, cycloramas were dome-shaped or horizontally curved, but may now also be flat or vertically curved as well. |
| **Cyclorama Light (Cyc Light)** | A luminaire mounted at the top and/or bottom of a cyclorama in order to light it in a smooth, uniform manner. |

| | |
|---|---|
| **Daylight** | Light that has a color temperature of approximately 5500 - 5600° K, which has been approximated to be the color temperature of ordinary sunlight during the day under normal atmospheric conditions. |
| **Daisy-Chaining** | Connecting items of equipment together by linking from one to the next in a chain. |
| **Dichroic Color Filter** | Color filters manufactured by vacuum depositing thin films onto heat resistant glass. Dichroic filters reflect rather than absorb unwanted wavelengths and so remain cooler and less subject to burn out. The process for creating dichroic filters is very precise and much more saturated (purer) colors can be created. As a result, these filters are quite expensive and are used primarily in automated fixtures. |
| **Dimmer** | A device that causes connected lamps to decrease in intensity. Most dimmers for entertainment lighting use are some variation of an SCR (Silicon Controlled Rectifier). Individual dimmers are traditionally arranged in modules of two dimmers with modules combined into dimmer racks. |
| **Dimmer Rack** | Dimmer racks contain individual dimmer modules arranged for convenient electrical connection. Some racks are designed for permanent installation, while touring racks are designed for portable use. Dimmer racks typically contain 6, 12, 24, or 48 dimmer modules typically with 2 dimmers per module. |
| **Distribution Board (Distro)** | System of interconnected fuse carriers and cabling that routes an incoming power supply to a number of different outputs. |
| **Down Light** | 1. Downward illumination almost perpendicular with the floor. <br> 2. A luminaire that provides such illumination. |
| **Dry Ice Fogger (Fog Machine)** | A simple fog machine that creates thick, opaque, low-lying, or ground fog by the immersion of frozen $CO_2$ in hot water. This type of fogger is often made from a large drum containing a heating element and some type of basket in which dry ice can be lowered into the water. The resulting fog is often forced through a hose to the desired location onstage. Dry ice fog effects are somewhat short-lived as the dry ice quickly |

evaporates and the water cools. Dry ice is often used to cool the fog produced by other types of fog machines making it stay close to the ground. These chiller modules or attachments are little more than insulated coolers attached to the output end of a standard fog machine.

**Ellipsoidal or Ellipsoidal Reflector Spotlight (ERS) or Leko**

The most sophisticated of conventional instruments. Its beam shape is uniform, and various lenses inside the changeable barrels control the size of the beam. The unit is focusable so that an image can be projected and framing shutters allow the beam to be shaped to eliminate light spill onto projection screens, the audience's eyes, and such. The lens trains available range from very wide (50 degrees) to very small (5 degrees). Options include irises to further reduce the beam spread, to rotating pattern holders to make the projected images spin. This is the best instrument to use with gobo patterns. Usually 100 to 1000 W and throw distances of 10 to 100 ft.

**Effects Projector**

1. Animation Disc. A slotted or perforated metal disc that rotates in front of a lantern to provide "movement" in the light. Most effective when used in front of a profile carrying a gobo.

2. Effect Disc. A painted glass disc rotating in front of an effects projector with an objective lens to focus the image (e.g. Flames, Rain, Snow).

3. Flicker Flame. Irregularly slotted rotating metal disc through which light is shone onto a prism-type piece of glass which scatters the beam of light and adds the "dancing" effect of firelight to a scene.

4. Gobo Rotator. Motorized device inserted into the gate of a profile lantern that can be remotely controlled to rotate a gobo, usually with variable speed and direction.

5. KK Wheel. Slotted metal disc that rotates in front of a lantern to break up the light and provide movement (Flicker Wheel).

6. Lightning. Created through the use of either strobe sources or photoflood lamps.

7. Tubular Wave Ripple. Horizontal linear lamp around which a slotted cylinder is rotated providing a rising light (as reflected from water onto the side of a ship).

**Even Field**    A field that has a relatively uniform decrease in intensity as viewed from the center to the edge of the field (i.e. a field that does not have a noticeable hot spot).

**Fade In**    The gradual increase in intensity of light.

**Fade Out**    The gradual decrease in intensity of light.

**Fade To Black (FTB)**    A lighting design abbreviation. It indicates that a light cue takes all channels to zero over a period of time.

**Fader**    A vertical slider that is used to remotely set the level of a lighting channel.

**Feeder Cable**    The cable which feeds or supplies power to a dimmer rack. Feeder cable is usually heavy gauge cable capable of safely carrying the hundreds of amps necessary to supply as many as 96 individual dimmers in a rack. Feeder cables are usually connected via Camlock connectors. A bare-end or tail often connects one end of a feeder to the power supply or company switch.

**Fill Light**    1. Supplementary illumination used to reduce shadows, preventing them from appearing black.

2. A luminaire that provides such illumination.

**Fixed Focus**    A term used to describe an optical system whereby the lenses in a luminaire remain at a fixed distance from one another, although they may move as a group within the system.

**Fixture**    Used to describe a type of moving light.

**Flagging**    When focusing lighting, flagging means waving your hand in and out of the beam of a luminaire/instrument in order to see where the beam is hitting on stage.

**Flood**    1. The position of a movable lamp, lens, or pair of lenses on a spotlight that produces the widest field angle.

2. To direct a large amount of light on a relatively large area.

| | |
|---|---|
| **Flood Light** | A luminaire consisting of a reflector, lamp, and sometimes a single lens, used to direct a large amount of light on a relatively large area. |
| **Flown or Flying** | Suspending a lighting rig (trussing plus lights plus connectors and cabling) from hanging points in the ceiling using chain motors. The truss can also support audio systems. It is the cleanest and most effective means of setting up lighting and sometimes audio gear, in that it allows more flexibility in lighting, provides better sound quality, and eliminates sight line interference. It is usually more costly than ground supporting. |
| **Fluorescence** | A process by which certain pigments or materials can be made to appear to self-illuminate when exposed to UV light. |
| **Fly-Away** | A lighting design term referring to a cue in which automated lights move upward away from the stage in a sweeping motion. |
| **Focus** | The process by which a lighting instrument is either manually or remotely positioned to light a specific part of the stage. With conventional fixtures, focus is performed after lighting equipment is hung in place and is connected to the proper circuit. Automated fixtures can be remotely focused and may have many different focuses for a particular show. Focus presets are often created as libraries of focus points for a show. Focus presets as well as conventionally focused equipment must be checked any time a show changes venues, as the relationship between lighting instrument and stage may change. |
| **Focus Preset** | A feature of some automated fixture consoles that allows libraries of focus positions to be stored centrally in memory. Presets can then be accessed individually by cues to position fixtures at pre-determined locations on stage. Using focus presets is a much more efficient method for cueing automated fixtures than writing positions individually into every cue in a show. |

**Followspot**

A manually operated lighting fixture specially designed for following performers as they move about the stage. Most followspots employ some method for manual control of iris, shutter, dowser, as well as a color boomerang. Followspots can be either long-throw or short-throw instruments. The size of the room and the distance to be projected are the factors that determine the size and intensity of the unit to be used. Usually, they are 250 to 3000 W in power, and throw 50 to 200 ft.

**Framing Shutters**

Thin, movable, heat-resistant metal plates that are introduced into a beam such that a portion(s) of the beam is blocked off, (i.e. framed), affecting the beam pattern, usually forming a sharp edge in the beam. They are used in various types of luminaires, but extensively in ellipsoidal spotlights, usually four (top, bottom, right, and left), and followspots, usually two (top and bottom), always situated internally, and usually at the aperture. Framing shutters generally can be independently adjusted, but those used in followspots usually move simultaneously with a single control mechanism.

**Fresnel**

A standard stage lighting instrument. The Fresnel produces a characteristically intense, soft edged beam created by the pebbled surface on the back of the Fresnel lens. Excellent lighting for theaters, clubs and TV. Beam spread can be modified from flood to spot. Usually, they are 100 to 250 W with throw distances of 10 to 40 ft.

**Full Up**

A bright lighting state with all lights at "full" (100%) intensity.

**Gel**

A term used loosely to describe expendable color filters used in stage lighting. Originally made of thin sheets of dyed gelatin, color filters are now made from polymer plastics.

**Gel String**

A series of color filters connected end-to-end and used in a color scroller.

**Gobo**
Short for "go-between," and also called a pattern, template, or cookie, a gobo is commonly an etched steel cutout placed at the gate of an ERS that produces a pattern of light and shadow in the beam of light. Patterns are commercially available from theatrical lighting dealers or can be made by hand using a number of different processes. Many automated fixtures employ a variety of gobos and gobo effects. These include rotatable gobos, gobo combinations, glass colored gobos, or even sophisticated imaging systems which combine dichroic color effects with patterns or custom designs or artwork. For special events, company logos, names or other specific designs can be created as gobos.

**Gobo Holder**
A metal plate designed to hold a gobo of a particular size in a lantern of a particular type.

**Ground Support**
The truss, lifts, and towers that are set up at ground, stage, or platform level and used to support other truss or equipment above. They can be as simple as pipe and base structures (lighting tree) to large Genie lifts.

**Hang**
The lighting rigging session.

**Hanging Point**
The point where rigging is attached to a truss, or piece of scenery. Location of hanging points must be determined for structural safety, but must be reconciled with available pickup points in the building or structure to which the truss is being rigged.

**Haze Machine (Hazer)**
A device, similar to a fog machine, which produces a light, fine atmosphere by atomizing a special haze fluid. Since a haze machine does not utilize a heat exchange system, like a fogger, there is no warm-up time. The atmosphere produced by a haze machine is dense enough to reveal beams of light in the air, but not so dense as to become opaque

**Head**
1. A general term for a Fresnel spotlight.
2. The part of a followspot that contains the light source, (i.e. not the stand, ballast, or interconnect cable).

3. The part of a metal halide luminaire that contains the lamp, (i.e. not the ballast or interconnect cable).

4. The part of an ellipsoidal spotlight that contains the reflector, (i.e. not the lens barrel or the cap).

**High Intensity Discharge (HID)**  A type of lamp such as a mercury or sodium vapor lamp that produces light by causing an inert gas to discharge photons. HID lamps find special uses in entertainment lighting and make good UV sources. HID lamps require special ballasts and are generally not dimmable.

**Hot Spot**  The spot of light with the highest intensity, ideally located at or near the center of a beam that has been focused for a peak field.

**House Electrician**  The electrician employed by a facility who is in control of house lighting and any electrical or electronic equipment owned by the facility, or for which the facility is responsible.

**House Lights**  General venue lighting.

**Hue**  The red, orange, yellow, green, blue, violet, magenta aspect of color, without regard to other aspects such as saturation and luminance (i.e. the property of light that distinguishes it from gray of the same luminance).

**I.A.T.S.E (International Alliance of Theatrical and Stage Employees)**  A union representing professional craftspeople in the entertainment industry. This union includes stage electricians, carpenters, and projectionists. A venue is a union house if its local crew belongs to IATSE.

**Icon (TM)**  A moving yoke-type automated fixture distributed by Lighting and Sound Design (LSD).

**Indirect Lighting**  Illumination that falls on an area or subject by reflection, (e.g. bounce lighting).

**Instrument**  Lamp, lantern, or light.

**Intellabeam (TM)**  A moving mirror type automated fixture introduced by High End Systems/Lightwave Research in the late 1980s.

**Iris**  A device commonly used in an ERS or followspot to reduce the apparent diameter of the beam of light. Many automated fixtures also employ a motor-controlled iris that can be used to remotely adjust the beam diameter.

| | |
|---|---|
| **Jumper** | An adaptor from one type of electrical connector to another. |
| **Key Light** | A lighting design term that describes a strong primary light source. Other secondary lights are often described as being fill lights. The term "high key lighting" describes even bright lighting such as might be produced on a television news set. |
| **Kill** | To switch off (a light/sound effect) or to strike/remove (a prop). |
| **Lamp** | A device that converts electrical energy into light. Common lamps used in entertainment lighting include incandescent, HID, HMI/HTI, and fluorescent. |
| **Lampholder** | The electrical device that supports a lamp in a luminaire, and generally contains the contacts that make the electrical connection to the contacts of the lamp base. |
| **Laser** | Acronym for Light Amplification by Stimulated Emission of Radiation. A device that produces pencil-thin beams of coherent monochromatic light. Used primarily for special effects. Lasers combined with beam splitters, scanners, and mirrors, can be used to create a variety of three-dimensional images in fog or similar atmosphere. A laser and scanning system connected to a computer controller can be used to project complex animation effects. Great care is required when using lasers as this energy can cause permanent damage to the retina of the eye. |
| **Leko (TM)** | A trademark for a brand of ERS currently owned and marketed by Strand Lighting. |
| **Lens Barrel** | 1. The movable, inner tube of a focusing lens system in an ellipsoidal spotlight. |
| | 2. The complete tubular front section of an ellipsoidal spotlight that contains the lenses. |
| **Lens Holder** | 1. Any apparatus used to retain a lens. |
| | 2. See definitions #1 and #2 for Lens Barrel. |
| **Level** | 1. An abridged version of light level. |
| | 2. The position of a slider on a control console. |
| **Light Board** | A lighting control console or desk. |

| | |
|---|---|
| **Light Cue** | A lighting design term referring to a point in a show at which a predetermined change in the lighting is executed. The lighting director or stage manager "calls the cue" usually by saying "go," and the light board operator executes the lighting change. A change may occur instantly, as in a bump cue, or take place as a long fade over time. On simple controllers, a cue can be thought of as a combination of channels at specific levels which create the lighting for a specific moment in a show. More sophisticated controllers build cues in increasingly complex ways making the idea of a cue a more abstract concept. Cue is often used to describe a moment or picture (also called a look or state) created by lighting on stage. |
| **Light Board Operator (Board Op)** | The person who runs the lighting control console, programming and executing cues as directed by the lighting designer. |
| **Light Leak** | Unwanted light that escapes a luminaire from a location other than its intended opening. |
| **Light Level** | The average illumination on a subject, performing area, or part thereof. |
| **Light Show** | A term describing a production where the lighting takes a primary focus. The idea of a light show may have developed from the psychedelic light shows of the late 1960s, but is now used to describe a range of laser and lighting spectacles. |
| **Lighting Control Console** | The head end of a lighting system. The lighting control console sends information via control cables to dimmers or other devices instructing what they should do. Run by a light board operator, or as is common on a touring production by the lighting designer or lighting director, the lighting control console stores and executes all of the light cues for a performance. Common types of lighting consoles include the preset board and computer memory console. |

| | |
|---|---|
| **Lighting Crew** | A group of individuals trained in lighting skills and techniques, and collectively assembled to work on a stage, film, or video production. The group may include any or all of the following: stagehands, electricians, roadies, gaffers, grips, operators, and lighting technicians. |
| **Lighting Designer** | The person whose primary responsibility is the visual design of the lighting for a project or production. In theatrical terms, the Lighting Designer is responsible for all aspects of the aesthetic design of the show. |
| **Lighting Director** | Commonly used in the television and touring show industry to describe the person in charge of the lighting. Often the lighting director is the lighting designer for the production. In other cases, the lighting director for a touring show is working from an original production design by the lighting designer. |
| **Lighting Plot** | A scale drawing detailing the exact location of each lantern used in a production and any other pertinent information (e.g. its dimmer number, focus position, and color number). Often drawn from the venue floor plan. |
| **Lumen** | A unit used to measure the brightness of a light source. The more lumens produced per watt of power supplied, the more efficient a light source is. |
| **Luminaire** | The international term for lighting equipment. A complete unit for the purpose of generating usable and somewhat controllable light that comprises one or more lamps, parts designed to distribute the light, parts used to position and protect the light source, and a means to connect the light source(s) to an electrical supply. |
| **Mirror Ball** | A lighting effect popular in discos and ballrooms. A large plastic ball covered with small mirror pieces. When a spotlight (usually a Pinspot) is focused onto the ball, specks of light are thrown around the room. Usually motorized to rotate. |

| | |
|---|---|
| **Moving Mirror Automated Fixture** | A classification of automated fixtures, which achieve beam motion by reflecting the beam off of a remotely controlled, motorized mirror. The Cyberlight (TM) by High End Systems and the Roboscan (TM) by Martin, are examples of moving mirror automated fixtures. |
| **Moving Yoke Automated Fixture** | A classification of automated fixtures which achieves beam motion by remote motor controlled movement of the yoke and body of the fixture. The Vari-Lite (TM) series of automated fixtures is an example of moving yoke automated fixtures. |
| **Multicable (Mult, Multi)** | A cable designed to supply power from dimmers to multiple separate lighting instruments down a single multi-conductor cable. Standard multicables can carry the equivalent of 6 or 12 standard stage cables corresponding to the same number of circuits. A breakout is used at either end to break the multicable apart into individual circuits. Multicables have the advantage of being much smaller than bundles of multiple stage cables. |
| **Neon** | A type of discharge lighting generated by a high voltage across two oppositely charged electrodes at opposite ends of a long, thin glass tube filled with neon gas. As the electrical charge flows between the electrodes, electrons collide with neon atoms causing them to give off energy in the form of visible light. Different colors can be obtained by mixing other gases, or by using fluorescent coatings. For special events and advertising, the glass tube is bent to form letters and different shapes. |
| **Open Face** | A term used to describe luminaires that use no lenses. |
| **Operating Light** | A work light used by the operator of a control console. |
| **Outriggers** | Sturdy support legs that assist in stabilizing some stands and lifts. They are generally removable or easily folded away to assist in transporting or maneuvering the stand or lift. |

**Panelboard**

A piece of power distribution equipment comprising a box-like metal enclosure with a hinged cover, accessible only from one side, to allow access to internally mounted circuit breakers, switches, and fuses

**PAR or PAR Can**

A PAR can is comprised of a PAR (Parabolic Aluminized Reflector) lamp and a mounting fixture and base (the can). They produce a high intensity narrow beam of light. PAR lamps are available in many different sizes and powers. The bigger the number with a PAR Can, the bigger its size. Electric lamps used in PAR lamps are sized by multiples of 1/8 in. Therefore, a PAR8 (if such exists) would have a 1 inch diameter glass envelope. A PAR64 is 8 in. in diameter. To convert the PAR number to inches, divide the lamp number by 8. Some common PAR lamp types are:

1. PAR36. Practically all the PAR36 fittings are standard disco pinspot type with the very narrow beam 6 V, 30 W bulb. The most typical bulb used is VNSP bulb type 4515, which has 5 degrees beam and uses 6 V, 30 W. The PAR36 cans almost always have a transformer built in, and the bulb has screw terminals on the back. There are also other more rarely used special PAR36 lamps (12 V models, up to 100 W models, etc.).

   The PAR36 lamp diameter is 4.3 in. (around 110 mm). PAR36 lamps come in a mega range of oddball voltages and powers for things like marine and aircraft (for example 28 V ACL version). Generally PAR36 lamps are a bit short-lived on continuous duty.

2. PAR38. PAR38 lamp diameter is around 4.75 in. (around 120 mm). These types of bulbs have typically an ES Edison Screw cap. Typical lamp power levels available are 60, 75, 80, 100, 150 and 300 W. Typical beam spreads

are 30 and 60 degrees (special 12 degree bulbs exist also). These types of lamps are common in shop display fittings and security lights, also in outdoor garden lighting (special bulb version for outdoor use).

3.  PAR46. PAR46 lamp diameter is around 5.75 in. (around 146 mm). Typical lamp power is around 200 W. Bulb has blade connectors.

4.  PAR56. PAR56 lamp diameter is around 7 inches (around 178 mm). Typical lamp power is 300 W. Bulb has blade connectors. Typical beam spread is 11 x 25 degrees. Different beam spreads are available. PAR56 lamps are typically available at 300 W and 500 W power.

5.  PAR64. PAR64 lamp diameter is around 8 in. (around 203 mm). Typical lamp power is 500 W or 1000 W. Bulb has blade connectors. Typical beam spread is 11 x 25 degrees. Different beam spreads are available.

6.  PAR Cans serve many purposes in special events including décor lighting (e.g. up walls) and stage washes

**Patching**

1.  To cross-connect lighting circuits around the stage area to a chosen dimmer. Connecting lanterns to dimmers.

2.  Using a cross-connect panel that enables any stage lighting channels to the control desk to control any dimmer or group of dimmers. Some large lighting boards have the facility for soft patching, a totally electronic way of patching. Some Rock Desks have a pin patch, which allows groups of dimmers to be allocated to a particular control channel.

**Photoflood**

Lamp used by photographers that gives a bright white light. Because it has a thin filament, it gives a good flash effect (e.g. lightning), but has a relatively short life, so should not be left on for any length of time.

**Pick up**

The action of turning a followspot on a performer.

| | |
|---|---|
| **Pickup Point (Pick Point)** | An architectural or structural point to which scenery or trussing can be rigged for flying purposes. Available pickup points in a particular venue must be reconciled with necessary hanging points on the equipment to be lifted. |
| **Pinspot** | A spotlight that has an extremely narrow beam, frequently used to illuminate and isolate table centers. It is controllable only by aiming it where it is wanted. Usually 75 to 1000 W with a throw of 5 to 50 ft. |
| **Pre-Hung Truss** | A truss or truss section which has been pre-assembled with lighting equipment and connecting devices in the shop prior to installation at load-in. Using a pre-hung truss saves many hours when loading a show in or out, and makes for an efficient method of storing equipment on a truck. |
| **Preset Board** | A lighting control console comprised of banks or "scenes" of redundant sliders each controlling one channel of the lighting system. Individual looks can be set up on banks and by using scene masters one look can be faded to the next. The two-scene preset is the most common preset board. Cues are manually set on alternate scene banks and faded from one to the other. Multi-scene preset boards can also be found in some permanent installations, which can require multiple operators to preset. |
| **Punch Light** | A high intensity luminaire that floods an area with light whose color temperature is approximately that of daylight. |
| **Programming** | The process by which light cues are setup, written, and recorded into memory on a memory console. Programming on contemporary control consoles may involve complex manipulation of functions and software, but rarely involves actual program coding. |
| **Protocol** | The specific type of analog or digital signal, AMX or DMX512, used by a control console and the equipment it controls. |
| **Quad-Box** | A piece of power distribution equipment comprising a small, metal enclosure housing four, flush, female connectors, and a permanently installed power cord whose conductors are electrically connected to the female connectors. |

| | |
|---|---|
| **Rack** | An abridged version of Dimmer Rack or Power Distribution Rack, or an apparatus that is a combination of the two. |
| **Rated Lamplife** | The total length of time that a lamp should operate effectively, as set by the manufacturer. |
| **Reflector** | 1. Generally, anything that causes reflection. |
| | 2. A metal or glass apparatus, usually curved in some manner, used in most luminaires for the purpose of directing light rays from a light source. |
| | 3. In the film and video industries, a metallic or reflective fabric panel, used for bounce lighting, or simply to redirect light, with the light source being a luminaire or sunlight. They are available in a variety of sizes and shapes, and materials of varying reflectance. |
| **Response Time** | 1. The time it takes for a dimmer to reach its intended level from the initiation of an input control signal. |
| | 2. The time it takes a lamp filament to react to a change in voltage. |
| **Rig or Rigging** | 1. A complete structural assembly for hanging or supporting luminaires, scenery, and/or other production equipment comprising some or all of the following: truss, motors, support cables, clamps, pulleys, pipes, and other hardware, for the purpose of creating a somewhat portable and temporary performing area. |
| | 2. To set up and connect support items, such as cables, ropes, pulleys, hoists, motors, chains, or slings between the points and the items to be flown. |
| **Rigger** | A technician chiefly responsible for the rigging for a tour or production. |
| **Road Case** | Sturdy, rugged box, often supplied with handles, and castors or wheels, used to transport and protect production equipment such as control consoles, dimmer racks, luminaires, and related equipment. |
| **Road Crew** | Technical crewmembers who travel with a production on tour. |
| **Runway Lights** | Footlights that are used on stage runways. |

| | |
|---|---|
| **Roboscan (TM)** | A moving mirror automated fixture manufactures by Martin. |
| **Rolling Rack** | A portable dimmer rack on castors for ease of transportation. |
| **Safety Cable** | A steel cable that has a clip on one end and a loop on the other. It is intended to be threaded through a piece of hanging equipment and around a support structure, such as a batten or truss, and then clipped to its loop. It then acts as a safety support should the primary support, such as a pipe clamp or hanging arm, fail. |
| **Scene or Scene Preset** | 1. A set of predetermined light levels that can be set up on a control console in advance of need, and to which the operator may fade or go to when desired.<br>2. A term used to describe a control console that has such a capability. |
| **Scoop** | Named for its scoop-like shape, an open face flood light with a large, diffused reflector that is essentially the body of the luminaire. The reflector is parabolic, spherical, or ellipsoidal, and is generally made from unpainted aluminum. |
| **Scrim** | In the theater and special events industry, a thin, gauze-like curtain. When illuminated from the front, it appears opaque, and when illumination is present behind it but not on it, the scrim becomes almost transparent. It can also appear translucent when there is some illumination directly on it, and some illumination present behind it, in the proper proportions. |
| **Sealed Beam Lamp** | A lamp with an integral light source, reflector, and lens, all of which are either sealed within, or are part of the envelope. |
| **Sharktooth** | A material used for fabric scrims used in theater. |
| **Shin Buster** | 1. A luminaire placed as close to the stage floor as possible. It is focused such that no light shines on the floor, thus giving the illusion that the subject is floating.<br>2. Generally, any luminaire mounted close to the stage floor. |

| | |
|---|---|
| **Short Throw** | A term used to describe a luminaire that has an effective intensity at a relatively short distance. This term is very subjective and dependent on the type of luminaire used. |
| **Shutters** | 1. An abridged version of Framing Shutters.<br>2. A rectangular, metal apparatus that resembles a Venetian blind in form and function, generally used as a mechanical dimmer or blackout mechanism on large spotlights. |
| **Side Light** | Light which comes primarily from the side of the performer or object being lit. Strong side lighting is associated with the emphasis of the edges or sides of actors or objects, tending to enhance their dimensionality. |
| **Smoke Machine** | A Smoke Machine or Fogger is an electrically powered unit that produces clouds of white non-toxic fog (available in different flavors/smells) by the vaporization of mineral oil. It is specially designed for theater and film use, but often finds its way into special events. |
| **Socapex (TM)** | A multipin connector that can carry a series of lighting or sound circuits. Very robust and designed for touring. Available in 19-pin (6 circuits) and 37-pin (12 circuits) configurations. Sometimes shortened to SOCA. |
| **Soft Light** | 1. Illumination that produces shadows with a soft edge.<br>2. A luminaire that provides such illumination. |
| **Soft Patch** | A term used to describe a patch system whereby the dimmers can be interchangeably assigned to any one of any number of channels. This type of patch system is usually found on memory boards. |
| **Solo** | On a lighting console, Solo mode kills all other channels except the single dimmer you're working with. It can be useful for identifying a channel in a large rig, but can be dangerous during a show. Some consoles allow you to assign flash buttons to Solo mode that will turn off all channels except those loaded into that flash button or submaster. |
| **Source Four** | Range of luminaires manufactured by ETC. |

| | |
|---|---|
| **Special** | A luminaire within the lighting rig that is required for a specific moment or effect within the performance and is not part of the general cover lighting. |
| **Spill** | Unwanted light onstage. |
| **Stage Wash** | See Wash. |
| **Star Cloth (Drop)** | A piece of scenic canvas, painted or plain, that is flown or fixed to hang in a vertical position, usually black, and has a large number of small low-voltage lamps sewn or pinned through it which gives a magical starry sky effect. |
| **Strobelight** | A special lighting effect that produces multiple rapid bursts of high intensity light. Strobe lighting is almost always produced by a compact xenon strobe lamp activated by a power supply and timing circuitry. Strobelights can be simple low power devices with fixed flash rates, or sophisticated devices triggered by a lighting control console at specific intervals. |
| **Telescoping Stand** | A height-adjustable stand that has two or more concentric tubular sections, (e.g. risers), that slide inside one another and lock into place. |
| **Three-Fer** | A circuiting device that allows three lighting instruments to be joined into one cable or circuit. |
| **Three-Phase** | 1. A term for an alternating current electrical supply that has three hot legs, with each leg at a phase that is 120° apart from the other, with or without a neutral leg. <br> 2. A term used to describe something that requires a three-phase electrical supply to operate. |
| **Throw Distance** | The effective distance between a luminaire and the area or subject to be illuminated. |
| **Tie-In** | To connect the line side leads of power distribution equipment, dimmer racks, etc., to the primary electrical supply for a location, such as a company switch, circuit breaker panel, or other piece of power distribution. This is generally done with feeder cables. |

| | |
|---|---|
| **Tie-In Set** | A set of feeder cables or other necessary connecting devices needed to tie-in a dimmer rack. A standard tie-in set includes a ground, neutral, and three hot cables with bare-ends in one end for connection at the company switch or disconnect panel. |
| **Trim** | 1. To finely adjust the height of battens, curtains, or any item whose exact height is critical. |
| | 2. To finely adjust the voltage output of some electronic dimmer at the lowest control setting. |
| | 3. To finely adjust the focus, beam direction, shutter positions, etc., for a group of luminaires set up for a production. |
| **Truss** | A framework of alloy bars and triangular cross-bracing (usually of scaffolding diameter) providing a rigid structure, particularly useful for hanging lights where no permanent facility is available. Very often box-shaped in cross section, so known as Box Truss. This type of truss is useful for touring as luminaires/speakers etc., can be hung inside the truss which protects them when loading and takes up less space in the truck. Also comes as triangle truss but this has the disadvantage over box truss that instrumentation must be struck from the truss before it can be loaded into a truck. |
| **Twist-Lock Connector** | A commonly used type of locking blade connector that requires a twisting action to lock the mating connectors together, manufactured by Harvey Hubbel, Inc. The name "Twist-Lock" is trademarked. |
| **Two-fer** | An electrical connecting device that allows two lighting instruments to be combined into one cable or circuit. |
| **Ultraviolet (UV)** | An ultraviolet light source is used to create special lighting effects with fluorescent materials. UV sources can be incandescent, fluorescent, or preferably HID lamps. |
| **Union House** | A venue that is a union house holds a collective bargaining agreement with its union employees guaranteeing such things as pay scale, working hours and conditions. If a theatrical venue is a union house it is most likely covered by I.A.T.S.E |

| | |
|---|---|
| **Uplighting** | Cost-effective way in which to highlight décor pieces, accentuate given attributes of a venue, or just to add color to an event space. Typically used to light walls from floor-mounted light racks. |
| **Vari-Lite (TM)** | A company that manufactures, rents, and supports a complete automated fixture and control system. A pioneer in automated fixture technology, Vari-Lite supplies its own console operators and repair technicians for most applications. |
| **Wash** | 1. An even, overall illumination over a large area, typically a stage. |
| | 2. To create such an illumination. Can be a variety of things from three-color to one color, color-corrected, or video level lighting wash. Often described in terms of "K". Three-color or four-color is a basic wash for entertainers. It has different colors to set the mood for the performance. Video level lighting is a diffused white wash used for TV applications. "K" refers to thousands of watts of light. Thus, a 12 K, three-color wash is 12 instruments total in three groups of color, four instruments each, with each one rated at 1000 W. |
| **Wattage** | The measurement of the amount of power used by an electrical device. Stage lighting equipment is rated in watts (or Kilowatts, 1 kW being equal to 1000 W). This refers to the amount of power required to light the lamp. A higher wattage lamp requires more power and gives a brighter light output. Dimmers are rated in terms of their maximum load capacity in wattage. (Wattage = Amperage x Voltage) |
| **WYSIWYG** | Acronym of "What You See Is What You Get." Mainly used in the context of a software tool for lighting design and production administration. Capable of stunning 3-D rendering of lighting states, and direct connection to a lighting control desk. Enables accurate pre-visualization of lighting designs and greatly increases the understanding between director/producer and lighting designer in the early stages of a production. |

| | |
|---|---|
| **Xenon** | High output discharge lamp commonly used in Strobe lighting. Some followspots also use Xenon lamps. Xenon lamps have a color temperature of between 5600 to 6500° K. |
| **Yoke** | A sturdy, U-shaped metal bracket that attaches to opposite sides of a luminaire, or, video and film industry reflectors, butterflies, etc., such that it allows either to tilt freely. A locking mechanism is provided to prevent slippage when the desired position has been achieved. Also provided at the center of the yoke is a hole, stud, or receiver for mounting the yoke. |
| **Zoom Focus** | A term used to describe an optical system whereby the lenses in a luminaire adjust such that a beam pattern with a hard edge can be attained at various sizes at various distances without sacrificing beam lumens. |

# 13

## Audio

Whenever an event has more than a bare minimum number of people in a small room (e.g. maybe 100 people maximum, probably far fewer!), there will be a requirement for sound augmentation in order that any speeches or entertainment can be heard. Poor sound quality can be catastrophic for an event, especially if an important speech cannot be understood or a high-cost celebrity artist's sound mix is totally inadequate. Planners need to be aware of at least the basic elements of proper audio for events. Some of the following guidelines and comments are courtesy of Ajay Patil, Jay Rabbitt, and Doc Waldrop[5], in combination with my own experience.

To begin understanding audio, there are several factors that must be examined:

- Indoor or outdoor event
- Size of the event space
- Ceiling height and other room dimensions
- Acoustical characteristics of the space, including ceiling, wall and floor surface materials
- Number of people attending (seated or standing)
- Seating arrangements
- Room layout (i.e. event floor plan)
- Whether speakers can be flown (i.e. rigged from ceiling) and location of hanging points
- Purpose to which audio system will be put.

All of the above factors play a part in determining the extent and type of audio system to be used and thereby the cost. If it is an outdoor event, it can be considerably more complex to set up due to weather and power constraints. Often, an extra power generator must be brought in. If it is a large concert-type setup, there will have to be special audio towers constructed with protective weather covers, probably both for speakers and for the audio console. If the event is indoors, the complexity is less but the other factors still remain.

Audio falls into two main categories for special events:

# AUDIO FOR SPEECH

Often if speech is the main component of an event, the audio used takes on a different appearance than that for a concert or entertainment stage show. What is called a "distributed system" is most often used for speech. This type of system consists of multiple smaller speakers on stands distributed usually around the periphery of the event space. This permits clear sound coverage throughout the audience. It presents a more appealing and unobtrusive look to the equipment, and one that does not block sight lines. It is also better suited to improving the sound quality in acoustically challenging spaces with a lot of hard, reflective surfaces (e.g. glass-walled buildings).

# AUDIO FOR ENTERTAINMENT

Most entertainment, particularly musical acts and bands, utilize speaker stacks that incorporate lower frequency "bins." These systems tend to be large, cumbersome, and intrusive to sightlines. Therefore, they usually perform better "flown" or rigged from the ceiling if the venue structure and setup times permit. Both sound quality and sight lines are improved by doing this. If the event space is large with an audience that goes a distance back from the stage, delay speakers are also needed to compensate for the time delay in the sound reaching the rear of the audience. These can be either flown (better) or distributed as for speeches.

In addition to the larger speaker groupings, musical entertainers usually require a monitor system so they can hear themselves and the other musicians play. This system may be quite complex. It consists of a number of different monitors and "mixes" which combine certain performers and instruments into one monitor. The monitor board is normally positioned beside the stage.

The "house" or main audio console should be placed towards the rear of the event space and centered on the stage for the best results and for the audio engineer to hear properly. The cable or "snake" carrying all the audio inputs to the console from the stage must be either flown or taken around the periphery of the room. Note that it should be run either over doors, which is preferable, or along the floor, which means that in heavily used foot traffic areas (doorways), it must be covered with a solid cable cover or taped rubber mat.

# WHAT DOES THE AUDIO SYSTEM INCLUDE?

An audio system typically includes three groups:

## Input Group

This includes microphones, direct input boxes (DIs), keyboard mixers, and similar equipment inputs, which are all connected to a common onstage connector or junction box. This box forms one end of the "snake" or cable between the stage and the second group.

## Signal Processing and Routing Group

This forms the audio console end of the "snake" and includes the house console or mixer and usually a house effects rack for special effects (e.g. delay). This group is in turn also connected to the third group via the "snake."

## Output Groups

This includes a frequency equalizer system for the main sound, power amplifiers, the main speakers, and the entire monitor system, also including equalization, amplifier, and stage monitors.

We have included, as Table 13-1, a glossary of some of the most used special event audio terminology to assist with your understanding of the field.

Table 13-1: Glossary of Audio Terminology and Description of Equipment

| Term | Description |
|---|---|
| **AC (Alternating Current)** | Electrical current that alternates direction (positive to negative). AC is often contrasted with direct current (DC), commonly produced by batteries for portable equipment in the special events industry. AC is what is installed in buildings. |
| **Absorption** | The tendency of sound waves to be soaked up by soft surfaces. Opposite: reflection. |
| **Acoustics** | 1. The science or scientific study of sound. <br> 2. The properties of a room or environment that affect the qualities of sound. |
| **Acoustic Power Output** | The output, as measured in watts, of anything that generates sound. |
| **Acoustic Suspension** | A type of speaker cabinet that is sealed to control the action of its woofer and prevent the leakage of air. |
| **Acoustic Treatment** | Physical treatment of a room in order to change the room's acoustics, by using absorbers to attenuate the sound, reflectors to redirect the sound, and diffusers to uniformly distribute the sound. |
| **Ambiant Noise Level** | "Background" noise - from any source - that affects the listener's ability to hear what is produced by a sound system. |
| **Ampères, Amperage (Amps)** | Units of electrical current. |
| **Amplifier (Amp)** | 1. An electronic device that increases the amplitude of a signal. The signal may be voltage, current, or both (power). <br> 2. A combination speaker/amplifier designed for use with an instrument, as with a guitar amp or keyboard amp. |
| **Amplitude** | 1. The strength of sound waves or an electrical signal, as measured against a mean. <br> 2. That which determines loudness. |

| | |
|---|---|
| **Analog-To-Digital Converter (ADC)** | The electronic component that converts the instantaneous value of an analog input signal to a digital word (represented as a binary number) for digital signal processing. The ADC is the first link in the digital chain of signal processing. |
| **Anechoic** | 1. The complete absence of reflected sound (echo). |
| | 2. An environment that prevents (through dissipation or absorption of sound waves) all reflected sound, as in an anechoic chamber. |
| **Attenuate** | To make weaker. An attenuator uses resistance to reduce output voltage, as with a volume control. |
| **Automatic Mic Mixer** | A specialized mixer optimized for solving the problems of multiple live microphones operating together as a system, such as found in boardrooms, classrooms, courtrooms, church systems, or even hotel ballrooms. An automatic mic mixer controls the live microphones by turning up (on) mics when someone is talking, and turning down (off) mics that are not used. Thus it is a voice-activated, real-time process, without an operator, hence, automatic. |
| **Balance control** | A control found most commonly on professional and consumer stereo preamplifiers, used to change the relative loudness (power) between the left and right channels. |
| **Balanced Line** | A pair of ungrounded conductors whose voltages are opposite in polarity but equal in magnitude. Balanced lines reduce interference from external sources like radio frequencies and light dimmers. |
| **Bass** | The lower end of the frequency range, from about 20 Hz to about 300 Hz. |
| **Bass Reflex** | A speaker that, as a means of enhancing the efficiency of the reproduction of bass frequencies, channels some of the sound pressure generated by its woofer(s) through an opening (port) in its cabinet. |
| **Beltpack** | Part of the communication system (see **Clear-Com**) in an event, the beltpack contains the controls and circuitry to drive the headset worn by crewmembers. |

| | |
|---|---|
| **Biamplification** | The use of separate amplifiers to power woofers and tweeters. See: **Crossover - Electronic, Crossover - Passive.** |
| **Board** | Also control board. See: **Mixer, Mixing Console** |
| **Cable - Coaxial** | A single copper conductor, surrounded with a heavy layer of insulation, covered by a thick surrounding copper shield and jacket. A constant-impedance unbalanced transmission line. |
| **Cable - Fiber Optics** | Short distances (typically less than 150 ft) use plastic fibers, while long distances must use glass fibers. |
| **Cable - Mic or Audio** | A shielded twisted-pair, usually designed for low current, high flexibility and low handling noise. The best insulating materials are somewhat inflexible, so most mic cables use rubber, neoprene, PVC, or similar materials, with small gauge wire, and therefore, true mic cables are not intended for long runs. Unfortunately the term "mic cable" has become synonymous with general-purpose audio cable (as distinguished from speaker cable) when it can be quite different. The very best audio cable may not be the best mic cable and vice versa. |
| **Cable - Quad Mic** | A four-conductor cable exhibiting very low noise and hum pickup (hum reduction can be 30 dB better than standard mic cable). |
| **Cable - Speaker** | An unshielded insulated pair, normally not twisted, characterized by heavy (or large) gauge conductors (hence, low-resistance), used to interconnect the output of a power amplifier and the input of a loudspeaker. |
| **Cable - Twisted-Pair** | Standard two-conductor copper cable, with insulation extruded over each conductor and twisted together. Usually operated as a balanced line connection. |
| **Cardioid** | Heart-shaped pattern exhibited by some microphones that reduces pick up from the sides and back. |
| **Clear-Com** | Brand name of the most common type of communication equipment used for closed communication amongst technical crewmembers running an event. The equipment can be either wireless, enabling the crewmembers freedom of movement around the event space, or wired, requiring them to remain at a fixed position. |

| | |
|---|---|
| **Clipping** | Audible distortion that occurs when a signal's level exceeds the limits of a particular circuit. When an amp is "turned up too loud," and begins to distort, it is said to be clipping. |
| **Compact Disc (CD)** | Trademark term for the Sony-Philips digital audio optical disc storage system. The system stores 80 minutes (maximum) of digital audio and subcode information, or other non-audio data, on a 12 cm diameter optical disc. The disc is made of plastic, with a top metallized layer, and is read by reflected laser light. Variations (such as the "3 in." disc) are reserved for special applications. |
| **Compression Driver** | A driver, designed for use with a horn, which utilizes a diaphragm (rather than a cone) to reproduce mid and high frequencies. |
| **Compressor** | A device that reduces - compresses - a signal's dynamic range. Basically, it makes "loud sounds quieter and quiet sounds louder." Most often associated with a vocal microphone. |
| **Condenser Microphone** | A mic that depends on an external power supply (phantom power) or battery to electrostatically charge its condenser (capacitor) plates. The power comes from the microphone pre-amp or the mixing console. |
| **Conductor** | A substance - in electronics, usually a metal - that allows the free flow of electrons. |
| **Cone** | The vibrating diaphragm, employed in some speaker designs, that generates sound waves. |
| **Connector - Banana Jack** | A single conductor electrical connector with a banana-shaped spring-metal tip most often used on audio power amplifiers for the loudspeaker wiring. |
| **Connector - Binding Posts** | Alternate name for banana jacks above, derived from the capability to loosen (unscrew) the body and insert a wire through a hole provided in the electrical terminal and tighten the plastic housing down over the wire insulation, holding the wire in place. |
| **Connector - Cannon Connector** or **Cannon Plug** | Alternate reference for XLR. |

| | |
|---|---|
| **Connector - Elco**<br>**Connector** or **Elco Plug** | AVX Elco manufactures several connectors used for interconnecting multiple audio channels at once, most often found in recording studios on analog and digital audiotape machines. |
| **Connector – Euroblocks** | Shortened form of European style terminal blocks, a specialized disconnectable, or pluggable terminal block consisting of two pieces. The receptacle is permanently mounted on the equipment and the plug is used to terminate both balanced and unbalanced audio connections using screw terminals. |
| **Connector - RCA**<br>(also known as **phono jack** or **pin jack**) | The standard connector used in line-level consumer and project studio sound equipment, and most recently to interconnect composite video signals. |
| **Connector - Speakon®** | A registered trademark of Neutrik for their original design loudspeaker connector, now considered an industry standard. |
| **Connector - Terminal Strips** or **Terminal Blocks** | Also called barrier strips, a type of wiring connector provided with screwdown posts separated by insulating barrier strips. |
| **Connector - ¼ in. " TRS (tip-ring-sleeve)** | Stereo ¼ in. connector consisting of tip (T), ring (R), and sleeve (S) sections, with T = left, R = right, and S = ground/shield. |
| **Connector - ¼ in. TS (tip-sleeve)** | Mono ¼ in. connector consisting of tip (T) [signal] and sleeve (S) [ground & shield] for unbalanced wiring. |
| **Connector - XLR** | The standard connector for digital and analog balanced line interconnect between audio equipment. Also known as a cannon plug. |
| **Console** | A large or elaborate mixer. |
| **Critical Distance** | The distance from a sound source at which sound pressure levels emitted by the source equal those being reflected off other sources. |
| **Crossfade** | Within the pro audio industry, a term most often associated with DJ mixers and broadcast. DJ mixers usually feature a crossfader slide-type potentiometer control. This control allows the DJ to transition from one stereo program source |

(located at one travel extreme) to another stereo program source (located at the other travel extreme). It is the crossfader that becomes the main remix tool for turntablists.

**Crossover** An electrical circuit (passive or active) consisting of a combination of high-pass, low-pass, and bandpass filters used to divide the audio frequency spectrum (20 Hz to 20 kHz) into segments suitable for individual loudspeaker use. Since audio wavelengths vary from over 50 ft at the low frequency end, to less than 1 in. at the high frequency end, no single loudspeaker driver can reproduce the entire audio range. Therefore, at least two drivers are required, and more often three or more are used for optimum audio reproduction. Named from the fact that audio reproduction transitions (or crosses over) from one driver to the next as the signal increases in frequency. For example, consider a two-driver loudspeaker crossed over at 800 Hz. Here only one driver (the woofer - "woof, woof" = low frequencies) works to reproduce everything below 800 Hz, while both drivers work reproducing the region immediately around 800 Hz (the crossover region), and finally, only the last driver (the tweeter - "tweet, tweet" = high frequencies) works to reproduce everything above 800 Hz.

**DAT (Digital Audio Tape Recorder)** A digital audio recorder utilizing a magnetic tape cassette system with rotary heads similar to that of a video recorder.

**dB (Decibel)** A relative unit of measure between two sound or audio signal levels. A difference of 1 dB is considered to be the smallest that can be detected by the human ear. An increase of 6 dB equals twice the sound pressure.

**DC (Direct Current)** Electrical current that flows in only one direction.

**Delay**
1. A signal processing device or circuit used to delay one or more of the output signals by a controllable amount. This feature is used to correct for loudspeaker drivers that are mounted such that their points of apparent sound origin (not necessarily their voice coils) are not physically aligned. Good delay circuits are frequency independent,

meaning the specified delay is equal for all audio frequencies (constant group delay). Delay circuits based on digital sampling techniques are inherently frequency independent and thus preferred.

2. Musical Instruments. Digital audio delay circuits comprise the heart of most "effects" boxes sold in the instrument world. Reverb, flanging, chorusing, phasers, echoing, looping, etc., all use delay in one form or another.

3. Sound Reinforcement. Acousticians and sound contractors use signal delay units to "aim" loudspeaker arrays. Introducing small amounts of delay between identical, closely-mounted drivers, fed from the same source, controls the direction of the combined response.

**Diaphragm**

1. The radiating surface of a compression driver. Its vibrations emit sound waves.

2. The moving element of a microphone.

**Direct Box**

Also known as a DI box, a device that enables a musical instrument (e.g. guitar) to be connected directly to a mic or line-level mixer input. The box provides the very high input impedance required by the instrument and puts out the correct level for the mixer.

**Directivity**

The ability of a speaker or horn to direct sound to a given area that can be described by its directivity factor (Q).

**Dispersion**

The area throughout which the sound produced by a speaker is distributed.

**Distortion**

Any discrepancy between the source material and the sonic output of a sound system; a measure of unwanted signals. If a piece of gear is perfect, it does not add distortion of any sort.

**DVD**

Officially "DVD" does not stand for anything. It used to mean "digital versatile disc" - and before that it meant "digital video disc" (also once known as HDCD in Europe). A 12 cm (4.72 in.) compact disc (same size as audio CDs and CD-ROMs) that holds 10 times the information. Capable of holding full-length movies and a video game based on the movie, or a movie and its soundtrack, or two versions of the same movie - all in sophisticated discrete digital audio surround sound. The DVD standard specifies a laminated single-sided, single-layer disc holding 4.7 GB, and 133 minutes of MPEG-2 compressed video and audio. It is backwards compatible, and expandable to two layers holding 8.5 GB. Ultimately two discs could be bound together yielding two sides, each with two layers, for a total of 17 GB.

**Dynamic Microphone** A microphone design where a wire coil (the voice coil) is attached to a small diaphragm such that sound pressure causes the coil to move in a magnetic field, thus creating an electrical voltage proportional to the sound pressure.

**Dynamic Range** The difference between the softest and loudest extremes within an audio signal as expressed in decibels (dB).

**Dynamic Processing** The use of electronic devices to control the levels of audio signals and compress or expand their dynamic range.

**Effects Loop** Inputs and outputs that allow the sending of an audio signal to and from a signal processor such as a reverb unit, delay, gate, or limiter.

**Electret Microphone** A microphone design similar to that of condenser mics except utilizing a permanent electrical charge, thus eliminating the need for an external polarizing voltage (i.e. wireless).

**Equalizer** A device that permits the precise control of specific frequency ranges. To perform this operation is said to be equalizing (EQ) the frequencies.

**Expander** An electronic device that increases dynamic range by reducing a signal's level any time it falls below a specific threshold.

**Fader** A control used to fade out one input source and fade in another. The fading of a single source is called attenuation and uses an attenuator.

**Feedback** Feedback, the dreaded "sound man's (and sound woman's) curse," is caused by a regeneration of sound leaving a speaker and entering a microphone. This tone - a sustained shriek - is a self-perpetuating cycle that can be stopped by decreasing the volume.

| | |
|---|---|
| **Filter** | A device that removes unwanted frequencies or noise from a signal. |
| **Flat** | The state of an audio signal or tone whose frequency is unaltered by equalization. On most mixers and equalizers, flat is indicated by the tone controls being at dead center. |
| **Foldback** | The original term for monitors, or monitor loudspeakers, used by stage musicians to hear themselves and/or the rest of the band. The term "monitors" has replaced "foldback" in common practice. |
| **Frequency** | 1. The number of sound waves that pass a given point in one second. |
| | 2. The determiner of pitch. |
| **Frequency Response** | The range of frequencies that is reproducible by a speaker or electronic component. |
| **Front of House (FOH)** | This is the location where the main mixer is usually placed for sound reinforcement systems. Meant to differentiate the main house mixer from the monitor mixer normally located to the side of the stage. |
| **Gain** | 1. The amplification characteristic of an electrical or mechanical device |
| | 2. The amount of volume that may be achieved before acoustical feedback occurs. Typically refers to the signal (such as vocals) going into a microphone. |
| **Gang, Ganged, Ganging** | To couple two or more controls (analog or digital) mechanically (or electronically) so that operating one automatically operates the other, usually applied to potentiometers (pots). |
| **Gate** | An electronic device that increases dynamic range by cutting off a signal when its level falls below a specific threshold. |
| **Graphic Equalizer** | A multi-band variable equalizer using slide controls as the amplitude adjustable elements. Named for the positions of the sliders "graphing" the resulting frequency response of the equalizer. Only found on active designs. Center frequency and bandwidth are fixed for each band. |

| | |
|---|---|
| **Ground Lift Switch** | Found on the rear of many pro audio products, used to separate (lift) the signal ground and the chassis ground connection. |
| **Ground Loop** | A voltage difference developed between separate grounding paths due to unequal impedance such that two "ground points" actually measure distinct and different voltage potentials relative to the power supply ground reference point. |
| **Handheld Mic** | See **Wireless Microphones**. |
| **Headset** | A headphone and microphone combination used in a communications system with a beltpack. |
| **Headset Mic** | See **Wireless Microphones.** |
| **Hertz (Hz)** | A unit of measure that equals one cycle per second. |
| **High Pass Filter** | A circuit that discriminates between high and low frequencies and allows only the high frequencies to pass. |
| **Hiss** | Random high frequency noise with a sibilant quality, most often associated with tape recordings. |
| **Horn** | An acoustical transformer which, when coupled to a driver, provides directivity and increases the driver's loudness. |
| **Hypercardioid** | A narrower heart-shaped pick up pattern than that of cardioid microphones. |
| **Interrupted** or **In-Ear Foldback (IFB)** | An audio sub-system allowing on-air personnel ("talent") to receive via headphones, or ear monitors, the normal program audio mixed with audio cues from the production director, or their assistants. Can also be used as an in-ear monitor for musicians. |
| **Input/Output (I/O)** | Equipment, data, or connectors used to communicate from a circuit or system to other circuits or systems, or the outside world. |
| **Impedance** | The measure of the total resistance to the current flow in an alternating current circuit, expressed in ohms, as a characteristic of electrical devices (particularly speakers and microphones). Most speakers are rated at 8 ohms. Microphones are usually classified as being either high impedance (10,000 ohms or greater) or low impedance (50 ohms to 250 ohms). |
| **Inductance** | A circuit's opposition to a change in current flow. |

| | |
|---|---|
| **Input Overload Distortion** | Distortion caused by too great an input signal being directed to an amplifier or preamplifier. Input overload distortion is not affected by volume control settings and most frequently occurs when mics are positioned too close to the sound source. Input overload distortion is controllable through the use of an attenuator. |
| **Inverse Square Law** | The law that states that in the absence of reflective surfaces, sound pressure (or light) falls off at a rate inverse to the square of the distance from its source. In other words, every time you double your distance from the sound source, the sound pressure level is reduced by 6 dB. |
| **Jack** | A female input or output connector, usually for a mic or an instrument. |
| **Lavalier** or **Lavaliere Microphone** | A small electret microphone designed to be worn on a person. Lavalier (the final "e" is commonly dropped) mics are usually attached by clips rather than hung from a cord. See **Wireless Microphones.** |
| **Limiter** | A compressor with a fixed ratio of 10:1 or greater. The dynamic action effectively prevents the audio signal from becoming any larger than the threshold setting. It is a device that electronically controls or "limits" the peak levels of program material. |
| **Line Level** | A signal whose voltage is between approximately 0.310 volts and 10 volts across a load of 600 ohms or greater. |
| **Load** | Any device to which power is delivered. |
| **Loudspeaker - Dynamic** | The heart of a dynamic loudspeaker is a coil of wire (the voice coil), a magnet, and a cone The amplifier applies voltage to the voice coil causing a current to flow that produces a magnetic field that reacts with the stationary magnet making the cone move proportional to the applied audio signal. |
| **Loudspeaker - Electrostatic** | A thin sheet of plastic film is suspended between two wire grids or screens. The film is conductive and charged with a high voltage. The film is alternately attracted to one grid and then the other resulting in motion that radiates sound. For pro audio applications, dynamic loudspeakers dominate. |

**Low Pass Filter**  A circuit that discriminates between high and low frequencies and allows only the low frequencies to pass.

**Microphone**  An electroacoustic transducer used to convert the input acoustic energy into an electrical energy output. Many methods exist; see also **electret microphone, condenser microphone**, and **dynamic microphone.**

**Microphone Processor**  A device that, when installed between a mic and an amp or preamp, allows the manipulation of the signal originating at the mic.

**Mixer**  An electronic device that permits the combining of a number of inputs into one or more outputs. Mixers commonly provide a variety of controls (e.g. tone, volume, balance, and effects) for each "channel." Typically, mixers have between 8 and 64 input channels. See: **Board, Console.**

**Monitor**  A speaker or earphone dedicated to making it possible for a performer to hear - or monitor - his/her own performance.

**Monitor Mixer**  A mixer used to create the proper signals to drive the individual musician stage loudspeaker monitors. Also called foldback speakers.

**Musical Instrument Digital Interface (MIDI)**  Industry standard bus and protocol for interconnection and control of musical instruments, or of other devices by musical instruments. First launched in 1983, now generalized and expanded to include signal processing and lighting control.

**Noise Gate**  A device that attenuates a signal when the program level falls below a preset threshold. It controls unwanted noise, such as preventing "open" microphones and "hot" instrument pick ups from introducing extraneous sounds into the system.

**Ohm**  The basic measurement unit of resistance.

**Ohm's Law**  The law that states the relationship between current, resistance and voltage in an electrical circuit: Amperage times resistance equals applied voltage (e.g. $V = IR$).

**Omnidirectional**  Capable of picking up sound or radiating sound equally from all directions.

**Oscilloscope**  An electronic device that displays, on a video screen, a representation of an electrical signal.

| | |
|---|---|
| **Over-Equalization** | Adjustment of the tone controls on an equalizer to or beyond the point at which sound quality is adversely affected. |
| **Overload Light** or **OL Light** | An indicator found on pro audio signal processing units that lights once the signal level exceeds a preset point. |
| **PA** | Abbreviation for public address system. One or more speakers connected to an amplifier that may include a mixer and any combination of sound reinforcement devices. |
| **Pad** | An attenuator. |
| **Pan** or **Panoramic Control** | A control found on mixers, used to "move," or pan the apparent position of a single sound channel between two outputs, usually "left," and "right," for stereo outputs. At one extreme of travel the sound source is heard from only one output; at the other extreme it is heard from the other output. In the middle, the sound is heard equally from each output, but is reduced in level by 3 dB relative to its original value. This guarantees that as the sound is panned from one side to the other, it maintains equal loudness (power) for all positions. |
| **Parametric Equalizer** | A multi-band variable equalizer offering control of all the "parameters" of the internal bandpass filter sections. These parameters are amplitude, center frequency, and bandwidth. |
| **Passive Equalizer** | A variable equalizer requiring no power supply to operate. Consisting only of passive components (inductors, capacitors, and resistors), passive equalizers have no AC line cord. |
| **Patchbay** or **Patch Panel** | A flat panel, or enclosure, usually rack-mounted, that contains at least two rows of ¼ in. TRS connectors used to "patch in" or insert into the signal path a piece of external equipment. |
| **Patch Cord** | A short electrical cable used to connect individual components of a sound system. |
| **Personal Monitor** | A monitor that is small enough to be directed at a specific performer. |
| **Phantom Power** | Operating voltage supplied to a condenser mic by a mixer or external power source. |
| **Phase** | The relationship of an audio signal or sound wave to a specific time reference. |

| | |
|---|---|
| **Phase Shift** | The phase relationship of two signals at a given time, or the phase change of a signal over an interval of time. |
| **Pick up** | 1. Device which, when attached to an acoustic musical instrument, converts sound vibrations into an electrical signal. |
| | 2. A way of describing the directional sensitivity of a microphone. An omnidirectional microphone has equal pick up from all around, a cardioid microphone is more sensitive from the front, and a hypercardioid has very strong directionality from the front. A figure-of eight microphone picks up front and rear, but rejects sound from the sides. |
| **Pitch Tone** | A function of frequency. |
| **Polarity** | A condition that has two states (in or out) and is usually described in one of three ways: |
| | 1. Acoustical to electrical (microphone). Positive pressure at diaphragm produces positive voltage at pin 2 of XLR or at the tip of a ¼ in. phone plug. |
| | 2. Electrical to acoustic. Positive voltage into the "plus" terminal of a speaker causes the speaker's diaphragm to move forward (produces positive pressure). |
| | 3. Electrical to electrical. Positive voltage into pin 2 of an XLR plug produces positive voltage at the output (pin 2 of an XLR jack), at the tip of a ¼ in. phone jack, or at the red (plus) connector of a binding post (banana terminal). |
| **Potentiometer (Pot)** | A variable resistor (rotary or linear) used to control volume, tone, or other functions of an electronic device. |
| **Power Amplifier** | An electronic device that increases the volume of a signal. A basic unit of all sound systems. Power amps are typically connected to a preamp which provides controls for individual functions (e.g. level, tone, etc.). |
| **Preamplifier** | See: **Power Amplifier.** |

| | |
|---|---|
| **Pre Fade Level** or **Pre Fade Listen (PFL)** | This little button on a mixing console allows you to hear only that channel in the headphones when it is pressed. PFL can also be useful in identifying your off-key singers so you can turn them down in the house! |
| **Proximity Effect** | An increase in the bass response of some mics as the distance between the mic and its sound source is decreased. |
| **Radio Frequency Interference (RFI)** | Radio signals from external sources (e.g. cell phones) that invade and can be heard through, sound systems. |
| **Reflection** | A term that describes the amount of sound "bouncing" off hard surfaces. |
| **Rejection** | A microphone's ability to selectively exclude sounds coming from outside its pickup pattern. |
| **Reverb** | Any electronic or acoustical device designed to simulate, or capture, the natural reverberation of a large hard-surfaced (echoic) room, and mix it back with the original recorded sound. |
| **Router** | An audio device used to selectively assign any input to any output, including the ability to add inputs together. In this way, one input could go to all outputs, or all inputs could go to just one output, or any combination thereof. |
| **Sensitivity** | The sound pressure level directly in front of the speaker (on axis) at a given distance and produced by a given amount of power. |
| **Shield** | A metal enclosure that prevents electronic components from being affected by unwanted interference. Shielded speakers may be placed near a TV, for instance, because their magnets cannot affect the picture tube. |
| **Shelving** | The setting of the on-axis output of complementary drivers (woofers, mid-range, tweeters) to provide the desired frequency response. |
| **Sibilance** | A hissing sound, as coming from vocals into a microphone. |
| **Signal** | An electrical impulse. |
| **Signal-to-Noise-Ratio** | The ratio, expressed in dB, of an electronic device's nominal output to its noise floor. |

| | |
|---|---|
| **Slap Echo (Slapback)** | A single echo resulting from parallel non-absorbing (e.g. reflective) walls, characterized by lots of high frequency content. So-called because you can test for slap echo by sharply clapping your hands and listening for the characteristic sound of the echo in the mid-range. |
| **Snake** | A cable - often running between the stage and control board - that combines multiple lines; used to connect mics, instruments, and monitors to a mixer. |
| **Sound Level Meter** | A device that measures, in dB, the amplitude of sound waves. |
| **Sound Pressure Level (SPL)** | The measurement of the loudness, or amplitude, of sound, expressed in dB. |
| **Sound Reinforcement** | The use of electronic devices to reinforce, alte,r or increase the level of sound. |
| **Splitter** | An audio device used to divide one input signal into two or more outputs. Typically this type of unit has one input with six to 16 (or more) outputs, each with a level control and often is unbalanced. |
| **Subwoofer** | A large woofer loudspeaker designed to reproduce audio's very bottom-end, (e.g. approximately the last one or two octaves), from 20 Hz to 80 to100 Hz. |
| **Suppression,** also **Gain Suppression** | The term used to describe the technique of instantaneous reduction of a sound system's overall gain to control acoustic feedback, and thus reduce echoes. |
| **Sweet Spot** | Any location in a two-loudspeaker stereo playback system where the listener is positioned equidistant from each loudspeaker. The apex of all possible isosceles (two equal sides) triangles formed by the loudspeakers and the listener. In this sense, the sweet spot lies anywhere on the sweet plane extending forward from the midpoint between the speakers. |
| **Squawker** | A common nickname for a mid-range driver. |
| **Toe-in** | The degree to which the inside front edges of a pair of speakers are angled toward each other. Often used for better room coverage. |
| **Transducer** | A device that converts sound into electrical energy (a microphone), or electrical energy into sound (a speaker). |

| | |
|---|---|
| **Transformer** | A device that alters electrical current. |
| **Tweeter** | A speaker (driver) that reproduces only frequencies above a certain range, usually about 3 kHz. |
| **Unbalanced Line** | Cable that consists of one conductor and a shield. |
| **Unidirectional** | A mic that picks up sound primarily from one direction. |
| **Voltage Controlled Amplifier (VCA)** | An amplifier whose output is controlled by varying its voltage rather than by direct resistance (as with a potentiometer). |
| **Voice Coil** | Wire, usually copper, wrapped around a former (tubular core). When attached to a cone or diaphragm, surrounded by a magnetic field, and set into vibration by an alternating current, a voice coil causes a speaker to emit sound waves. |
| **Voltage** | The electrical pressure (electromotive force) of a current within a circuit. |
| **Watt** | 1. A unit of measurement that equals about 1/746 horsepower or enough electrical energy to perform one joule per second. A joule describes the energy of one Newton displaced one meter in the direction of the applied force. A Newton is the amount of force needed to accelerate one kilogram one meter per second. |
| | 2. One volt multiplied by one amp. |
| **Wedge** | A monitor speaker, in the shape of a wedge, designed to sit on the floor and be directed toward the performer(s). |
| **Woofer** | A speaker (driver) that reproduces only frequencies below a certain range, usually about 800 Hz. |
| **White Noise** | Analogous to white light containing equal amounts of all visible frequencies, white noise contains equal amounts of all audible frequencies (technically the bandwidth of noise is infinite, but for audio purposes it is limited to just the audio frequencies). |
| **Wireless Microphones** | Also known as radio mics, they operate as handheld, lavalier or headset (forehead, over-the-ear, or boom) types. They all incorporate a microphone, battery, transmitter, and aerial. The handheld types incorporate all components in the body of the microphone. With the other types, the microphone is placed near the mouth but the transmitter, aerial, and |

battery are in a separate small box that must be affixed to the performer somehow, such as on a belt. Wireless mics operate on two different signal frequencies, VHF (very high frequency), which is cheaper, prone to signal dropout, and of lower quality, and UHF (ultra high frequency), which is more expensive and has a higher quality signal.

**Y-Connector** or **Y-Cord**      A three-wire circuit that is star connected. Also spelled wye-connector. It is okay to use a Y-connector to split an audio signal from an output to drive two inputs; it is not okay to use a Y-connector to try and sum or mix two signals together to drive one input.

# 14

# Visual Presentation Technology

The "tag team" of audio and visual equipment (A-V) can sometimes be confusing because it covers so much. As a personal preference, I like to separate the two because audio, especially, can be totally different depending on its purpose for an event. As discussed above, the audio needs of a complex stage show with music and dance are very different from a meeting consisting mainly of speeches. That is why it has been separated out for the purposes of this book.

Although most A-V companies do definitely deal in audio systems - and they are excellent at combining these systems with complicated multimedia presentations - they sometimes are not as experienced on the audio side when it comes to mixing and planning for a stage show and for entertainment programs.

Thus, for this section we will confine the remaining A-V elements to just the "visual" ones. It is here that most good A-V suppliers are worth their weight in gold. Getting the right equipment for the job is a matter of asking the right questions and doing a lot of listening. The following are some of the main considerations:

## TYPE AND USE OF PRESENTATION

Will this visual presentation be strictly as support for speakers and education or will it be a full-blown creative multimedia extravaganza incorporating two or more different formats of visuals? Is the event a social one or an educational one or a combination? If it is part of a multimedia presentation, will it be used as part of an entertainment program and/or even part of an entire décor design scheme?

If an educational meeting and the presentation is primarily for speaker support, the chances are that there will be no more than one or two supporting screens designed either as part of a stage set or off to one or both sides of a stage. Occasionally, smaller monitors may be used throughout the venue depending on the venue design and ease of actually seeing the speaker and stage.

If the presentation is part of an entertainment program or décor design scheme, then the possibilities become endless, and limited only by budget. Frequently now, with the advent of high intensity projection systems, A-V is being incorporated into entertainment and décor design. For example, visual elements such as computer animations, slides, and video are easily projected onto fabric shapes, onto walls, and suspended from ceilings as part of an event décor design. Similarly, computers are being pre-programmed with PowerPoint presentations that incorporate slides and video in ever-changing combinations to augment stage shows of dance and music. In fact, technology is now at the point where virtually any computer-generated image can be used as either décor or in support of a multimedia presentation using a combination of special intelligent lights and computers.

# FORMAT OF PRESENTATION

What format will the presentation take? There could be any number of formats or combinations and you should know what they are and choose the most effective ones for your goals. These can include:

- Video playback support for speakers or for other multimedia shows in any or all the different video formats.
- Image magnification (IMAG), which requires one or more live video camera positions with operators to follow the event proceedings, which are in turn projected onto large screens for easy viewing. These have the option of also recording the proceedings by simply putting a tape into the cameras.
- Projection of overhead slides generally in support of speaker presentations.
- Projection of 35 mm slides.
- Projection of computer-generated presentations such as PowerPoint, animations, and CD or DVD presentations played from a computer.
- Projection of speaker or MC scripts.

# PROJECTION AND DISPLAY EQUIPMENT

Once the presentation format is known, there are multiple choices for projection and display equipment. Some options include:

## Projection Equipment

- LCD, CRT, and DLP video and data projectors
- 35 mm slide projectors and carousels
- Overhead projectors.

## Display Equipment

- Screens
- CRT or LCD monitors
- Plasma displays
- Video walls
- Teleprompters
- Fabric surfaces and venue walls or other surfaces.

# SETUP OF PRESENTATION

Once the use and format of the presentation is determined, the planner and A-V supplier must decide on the optimum equipment for the job, using combinations of the above projection and display options. In so doing, you will need to answer some detailed questions about the event:

- How many attendees and what is the room layout? If this is a classroom setting, then more people can be accommodated within the space and there will likely be no obstructions to sight lines, meaning that screens can probably go only at the front of the room. If a dining setup, then attendees will be facing all different directions and you may need to consider projecting to different locations in the room. If an event in multiple rooms simultaneously, then smaller TV monitors in each room might be appropriate.
- What size of projection system do you need? If there is a large spread-out audience, this means a larger screen size. Your A-V supplier will have formulas to calculate the correct size of screen for the size of room and audience.
- Will you be projecting using rear projection or front projection? Each of these types has advantages and disadvantages. Rear projection is better if a cleaner look is wanted; however, it normally requires 18 to 20 ft of clear space for projection behind the screen. Front projection takes up less space behind but necessitates a projector in front of the screen, which in turn takes up space in front. Both types of projection

can be flown from the ceiling thus eliminating the possibility of any interference by people walking in front of a projector and, in the case of front projection, eliminating any space crunch almost entirely.

- Are sight lines to the screens clear or is there a possibility of any obstruction caused by people walking in front of a projector or of table centers or architectural elements (e.g. columns) being in the projection path? If so, then a decision will have to be made to either change the projection system or the event design.
- Will presenters need computer support in the form of remote mouse control or cabling for laptop computers near the stage?
- Will a teleprompter be required for speaker or MC scripts and, if so, is there sufficient unobstructed space for it near the stage?
- If a video wall is being used, is there sufficient space to allow for a large enough wall for easy viewing and where exactly is the optimum location?
- If IMAG is being used, where will the camera(s) be placed in order to obtain a good picture yet cause minimal obstruction to audience sight lines?
- Is there appropriate technical support at the venue in the form of electrical power, ceiling hanging points with an acceptable load rating, easy and early room access?
- Is the budget sufficient to do the job?

## ACHIEVING OPTIMUM RESULTS

Of all the technical elements of an event, arguably the most complicated is audio-visual, particularly with the advent of elaborate computer presentations. To deliver a high-quality event with no "glitches" requires a lot of advance preparation and planning. As always, anticipation is the key. Think about the following when planning for extensive A-V as part of your event:

- Give the A-V company **all** the event details as outlined above.
- Allow sufficient time for setup.
- Double-check the equipment list and setup details.
- Go over all presentations personally along with the A-V provider and ideally the actual equipment operator, preferably days before the event.
- Rehearse the presentations if time allows, or at minimum obtain script copies and show running orders and rehearse cues with the A-V operator.
- Following all these steps will not guarantee success but it will definitely decrease the likelihood of any technical problems.

Table 14-1: Glossary of Visual Presentation Terminology and Description of Equipment

| Term | Description |
| --- | --- |
| **Active Matrix** | LCD display that uses a solid state device to control each pixel cell for a more quality image. |
| **ANSI** | American National Standards Institute. |
| **Antenna** | A metal structure or wire that picks up or transmits electromagnetic energy through space. |
| **Aspect Ratio** | Ratio of width to height of a screen or image. Most computer and video images have an aspect ratio of 4:3, HDTV uses 16:9, and SXGA uses 5:4. |
| **Baud** | Data transmission speed, 28.8K baud is 28,800 bits per second. |
| **Beta** | A type of ½ in. tape used for editing and recording video. Very high quality. |
| **Brightness** | Generally refers to the brightness of projection equipment expressed in lumens. See **Lumens**. |
| **Carrier** | A continuous (usually high frequency) electromagnetic wave that can be modulated by a signal to carry information. |
| **CD ROM** | Compact Disk Read-Only-Memory. Similar to audio CD but used for data storage. |
| **Character Generator** | (Trade name Chyron). A unit that enables the creation of letters, numbers, or other characters for use with videos. |
| **Closed Circuit Television** | Television signal carried, usually via microwave or coaxial cable, between two or more locations, but not broadcast for general reception. |
| **Codec** | Coder/Decoder. A device that converts an analog signal into and/or from a digital signal. |
| **Composite Video** | Combines vertical-horizontal synchronization signals, color and picture into a single signal line. |
| **Compressed Resolution** | An electronic method of reducing the resolution of a signal to operate on a lower resolution device. An example would be an LCD projector that has a maximum resolution of 800 x 600 pixels being used with a computer that is displaying |

1024 x 768 resolution. The image quality will be reduced when compressed.

**Convergence**  Alignment of red, green, and blue video guns to combine and produce a single color video display.

**Cross Talk**  The unwanted leakage of signal between supposedly independent channels.

**CRT**  Cathode Ray Tube or picture tube.

**CRT Projectors**  Used to project video and computer images as with LCD projectors but slightly older technology using three CRTs. Generally higher resolution but not as bright as LCD projectors. Work very well with computers of different resolutions. No zoom lens capability. They take longer to set up. Almost completely obsolete now.

**DAT**  Digital Audio Tape recorder/player.

**Decoder**  Device that reconstructs an encrypted signal so that it can be clearly received.

**DLP**  Digital Light Processing or Micro Mirror technology, used in some newer Video/Data projectors. The projection system is based on an optical semiconductor known as the Digital Micromirror Device, or DMD chip, invented by Dr. Larry Hornbeck of Texas Instruments in 1987.

The DMD chip is an extremely sophisticated light switch containing a rectangular array of up to 1.3 million hinge-mounted microscopic mirrors. Each of these micro mirrors measures less than one-fifth the width of a human hair, and corresponds to one pixel in a projected image.

When a DMD chip is coordinated with a digital video or graphic signal, a light source, and a projection lens, its mirrors can reflect an all-digital image onto a screen or other surface. The DMD and the sophisticated electronics that surround it are known as Digital Light Processing™ technology.

**DLP Projector**  Uses DLP technology as described above. Extremely high resolution, compatible with most computers, very bright and compact.

**Downlink**  Signal sent from a communications satellite to the earth.

| | |
|---|---|
| **Duplex** | Mode in which there exists two-way communications satellite transmission systems. |
| **DVD** | Digital Versatile Disk, similar to CD but has higher storage capacity. See also the definition in the Audio Glossary. |
| **Editing** | To "cut," alter, correct, or revise video. |
| **Encryption** | The process of encoding or "scrambling" television signals. Used in business and broadcast television so that unintended audiences are unable to view the signal. |
| **Fast Fold Screen** | Da-Lite brand that is assembled on-site to form front or rear projection screens. See **Projection Screen** below. |
| **Fiber Optics** | Technology in which a modulated beam of light carries information through a thin glass or plastic fiber. |
| **HDTV** | High Definition Television with aspect ratio of 16:9. |
| **IMAG** | Image magnification. Refers to the process of routing a live video image onto a projection screen. |
| **ISDN** | Integrated Services Digital Network. High speed Internet access, digital video, and voice. |
| **Interface** | Connection or isolation device such as connecting a telephone line to sound equipment. |
| **Interlaced** | Two horizontal video scans (odd, even) per video frame. NTSC is a 2:1 interlace system. |
| **Keystone** | Trapezoid distortion usually caused by the projector being located lower than the screen bottom. |
| **Laser Pointer** | Handheld device that projects a bright red light, typically used for manually pointing at a projection screen. |
| **LCD** | Liquid Crystal Display. The liquid crystal display consists of an organic liquid suspension between two glass or plastic panels. Crystals in this suspension are naturally aligned parallel with one another, allowing light to pass through the panel. When electric current is applied, the crystals change orientation and block light instead of allowing it to pass through, turning the crystal region dark. LCD monitors are typically found in laptop computers, or inside multimedia projectors. Most flat-panel desktop computer monitors are based on LCD technology. |

| | |
|---|---|
| **LCD Projector** | An electronic Video/Data projector for displaying video and computer images on a large projection screen. Most such current state-of-the-art projectors have excellent image quality, high resolution (XGA), zoom lenses, keystone correction, are very bright (see **Lumens** below), and are easy to set up. |
| **LCD Projection Panel** | A flat panel LCD device that is placed on an overhead projector to display video and computer images. |
| **Light Valve Projector** | Very bright projection system for theater size screens. |
| **Lumens** | Unit of light measurement (brightness) typically for projectors. For projecting in dark rooms and/or small screens, a projector with a lumens rating of 600 to 800 will probably suffice. For more brightly lit venues and in high ambient light conditions such as daylight, a lumens rating as high as 12,000 may be required. Generally, the higher the lumens rating, the more expensive the projector. |
| **Luminance** | Video imaging relative brightness. |
| **Lux** | Unit of light measurement typically for cameras. |
| **Monitor** | Used for video or computer display. Can use CRT, LCD, or plasma technology. Generally, monitors come in aspect ratios corresponding to standard video (4:3) or HDTV (16:9). 4:3 aspect ratio monitors vary in size from about 20 in. diagonal to 50 in. diagonal screens, and 16:9 aspect ratio monitors vary from 30 in. to 56 in. diagonals. This translates into viewing distances for the farthest person from the screens of about 8 or 9 ft for the smaller screens to about 18 or 20 ft for the larger screens. In other words, monitors are really only good for small audiences. Note that monitors come with a variety of features, two of the more important being direct video and audio inputs to lessen degradation in signals. |
| **Multimedia** | Any combinations of Video, Audio and Visual presentations. |
| **Non Interlaced** | Only a single horizontal video scan per video frame. |
| **NTSC** | National Television Standards Committee (North American Television uses NTSC standards). |

| | |
|---|---|
| **Overhead Projector** | Used for displaying 8½ x 11 in. transparencies on a projection screen. These units typically sit on top of a projection cart or a table and are front projection only. The focal length of the lens determines how far in front of the screen the projector must be placed. This distance varies from about 5 ft for a 10.5 in. focal length lens, to 11.2 ft for a 14 in. focal length lens, so this space must be considered in room setup plans. Lamp brightness of overhead projectors varies from about 2000 lumens to about 12,000 lumens. As with other projectors, larger screens and larger rooms require brighter projectors. LCD panels typically require a brightness minimum of about 4000 lumens. |
| **PAL** | Phase Alteration by Line; the color television broadcast standard for the UK, Germany, and many other nations. |
| **Parallel Port** | Computer input/output connection that transmits data multiple bits at a time (e.g. a printer). |
| **Pixel** | The smallest picture element making up the computer video display. |
| **Plasma Displays** | Basically a new form of computer and video monitor. Plasma monitors work much like CRT monitors, but instead of using a single CRT surface coated with phosphors, they use a flat, lightweight surface covered with a matrix of tiny glass bubbles, each containing the gas-like substance, plasma, and having a phosphor coating. Each of the "pixels" in this matrix is actually comprised of three sub-pixels, corresponding to the colors red, green, and blue. |
| | Plasma displays eliminate the need for high voltage deflection coils and the long neck of a CRT. In a flat plasma monitor, a digitally controlled electric current flows through the appropriate parts of the matrix, causing the plasma inside the bubbles to give off ultraviolet rays. These rays in turn cause the bubbles' phosphor coatings to glow the appropriate color. Advantages include their small size (very thin and lightweight) making them easy to hang on walls, high brightness, and stability. However, at present they are still very expensive. |

**Projection Screen**

Projection screens come in several forms:

1. Tripod. These are for front projection only. The fabric pulls up and out of a metal cradle. The base is a three-legged tripod. They are available only up to 8 ft x 8 ft in size and are best used for presentations in small rooms/ spaces with audiences under 150 people.

2. Fast-Fold. These consist of a fabric that snaps to a rigid aluminum frame. The screen can be used for front or rear projection depending on the type of fabric used. Legs can be adjusted to various heights and the screens can also be flown if required. They are available in sizes up to 30 ft in width.

Correct screen size is determined by using a general formula. Find the distance to the last row of seats and divide by 8 to determine the screen height, then apply the aspect ratio of the media you will be using to arrive at the screen width. Usually this is 3:4 for computer or video images. For example, if the last row of seats is 70 ft from the screen, then the height should be approximately 8.75 ft, or for the closest screen size, 9 ft. Using the 3:4 ratio will then give a screen width of 12 ft. Assistance is best sought from a qualified A-V company for more complicated circumstances.

Ensure that you consider the lighting conditions and projection source when choosing a screen as their surface materials and texture vary, with certain surfaces providing better results under differing conditions. It is best to consult an A-V expert.

**Real-time**

A term used to describe any system which operates such that input, processing, and output take place over a short period of time and without any long delays or storage of input or of intermediate or final results.

**Rear Screen Projection**

Locating the projector behind a translucent screen to be viewed from the front.

| | |
|---|---|
| **Resolution** | For computers, this refers to the number of pixels contained in the maximum screen viewing area, in other words the amount of detail that is seen in an image. For video, it refers to the number of lines per inch. |
| **RF Signal** | Signal sent via radio frequency. |
| **RGB** | Red, green, and blue are the basic light components that make up color TV and computer displays. |
| **Scan Rate** | Horizontal and vertical scan speeds, usually specified in Kilohertz or Hertz. |
| **SCSI** | Small Computer Systems Interface (scussy). Connection interface for computer peripheral equipment. |
| **Scanning** | The electronic process of moving an electron beam across the CRT surface. |
| **SECAM** | Systeme Electronique Couleur Avec Memoire, the television standard used in France and throughout the Eastern Block Republics. It has 625 lines and 25 frames per second. |
| **Serial Port** | Computer input/output connection that transmits data one bit at a time (e.g. Computer mouse). |
| **Simplex** | Transmission in only one direction. |
| **Slide Projector** | Used for displaying 35 mm and 2 in. x 2 in. slides on a projection screen. |
| **Switcher, Data** | Takes a video signal from any number of sources and adjusts it before sending it to a projection system. The source can be a camera or playback unit. Adjustments include raising or lowering the scan rate, boosting the line resolution to the highest possible level (e.g. SVGA to SXGA), and splitting the signal to send it to multiple projectors. |
| **Switcher, Video** | Allows for switching between video sources (e.g. two or more cameras, different video standards, computer playback) and effects. The latest technology is seamless with no obvious picture interruptions during switching. |
| **Sync** | Synchronization. Scanning signals that are used to keep the video display generator locked to the source. |
| **SVGA** | Super Video Graphics Array. Resolution = 800 x 600 pixels. |
| **SXGA** | Super Extended Graphics Array. Resolution = 1280 x 1024 pixels. |

| | |
|---|---|
| **VGA** | Video Graphics Array. Resolution = 640 x 480 pixels. |
| **Videoconferencing** | Linking of two or more groups via closed circuit satellite television. |
| **Video In** | Input video connection for an electronic device such as a VCR, female RCA jacks, or BNC. |
| **Video Out** | Output video signal from a device such as a VCR or Camera, female RCA jacks or BNC. |
| **Videotape Formats** | There are several different formats for videotapes: |

    1. VHS or SVHS (½ in.). Inexpensive and popular, used extensively for movies and home recording prior to DVDs.

    2. Hi 8 (8 mm). This is better quality than VHS and designed for low cost industrial use.

    3. U-Matic (3/4 in.). The standard for commercial use with good resolution.

    4. Mini DV. New high quality digital format gaining popularity for industrial use. Very small.

    5. Betacam/Betacam SP. The professional standard of extremely high quality but expensive.

    6. Digital Betacam. Higher quality than Betacam SP. Current standard for quality in digital video production.

| | |
|---|---|
| **Video wall** | High-end image display systems consisting of multiple monitors (cubes) placed in various configurations such as 2 x 2 (e.g. 4 monitors with an overall aspect ratio of approximately 4:3), 3 x 4 (e.g. 12 monitors with an overall aspect ratio of 16:9 or HDTV size), and almost any other combination desired. The monitors are especially constructed for this type of display, typically vary from 2 to 4 or 5 ft in depth, and are designed to be stacked together. The monitors use the same technology as found in other projection systems (e.g. CRT, LCD, or DLP). The technology basically takes video, digital data and/or computer graphics input and feeds it into a processor that manipulates and splits the signal to allow it to go to one or |

more monitors. Almost limitless possibilities are available for uniquely displaying the image or combinations of images. The advantages of a video wall include constant resolution and brightness no matter to what size the image grows.

**XGA**     Extended Graphics Array. Resolution = 1024 x 768 pixels.

# 15

# Catering

Food, glorious food! The largest component of many event budgets, especially private and corporate events, is usually food and beverage. It is really no wonder. As human beings, we sometimes approach the preparation, service, and consumption of food and beverages with almost religious fervor. Since special events are "special," we like to consider what goes into our bodies at these events as being out of the ordinary realm of what we are used to eating in our daily lives. A poorly prepared meal, inappropriate combination of foods, inferior wines, slow service, crowded seating, and a host of other potential problem areas can be an event disaster in the making. That is why a planner should be conversant with at minimum the basics of catering management. In planning for a meal or even a simple reception - before the proposal is written - a form used for determining catering requirements can be helpful. A sample is found at the end of this chapter. Some of the considerations include:

## TYPE OF SERVICE

Apart from a simple coffee or juice break during a meeting, the three main types of catering service most likely to be encountered by a planner during any special event are:

### Served Meal

This is generally the most formal type of service in that guests remain seated for the entire meal. Most served meals have between three and five courses on average, but are known to go as high as eight. This type of meal requires the most wait staff, usually in the ratio of approximately one waiter to 15 to 20 guests. A nice average would be one waiter per table if the table seats 10 or more. Because of the higher number of staff, a served meal is almost always the most expensive.

This type of meal service also requires more time. On average, each course takes approximately 20 to 35 minutes to complete, including service, eating and clearing. Salad and soup courses are at the lower end and entrees at the higher end, but the average works well for planning purposes when other elements of the event must be considered such as speeches and entertainment.

## Buffet Meal

Buffet service is usually considered as more casual than a served meal. Guests are only served beverages such as water, wine, and coffee and must serve themselves all the food courses from buffet tables. As a result, this type of service is both faster and less expensive. A complete buffet that includes all courses normally takes about one to one and a half hours to complete in its entirety. Because of this, it is often the best choice if the meal is part of a lengthy program of speeches and entertainment. It works very well for a continuous event in which planners might want guests to be active for the entire time. It also serves to encourage more mingling and interaction amongst guests.

## Standup Reception with Heavy Hors d'oeuvres

In our seemingly ever-accelerating society, eating is too often considered more a necessity than a luxury to be slowly savored and enjoyed. This has led increasingly to events that incorporate a standup reception and mingling to replace a more expensive served or buffet meal.

This type of event can include a number of different methods of "getting the food to the guests." Passed hors d'oeuvres and drinks by wait staff and small food and beverage "stations" are the most common. In our experience, we have found this type of catered event to be fraught with potential problems and sometimes the ensuing complaints are not worth the lower associated costs. Some concerns of which to be aware are:

- Location of food and beverage stations. They should be easily located for guests to find, in sufficient quantity, and located to distribute the guests evenly throughout the total event space. Otherwise, some are not used at all while others are over-used and have continuous lineups.
- Quantities of food and beverages. The expectation of guests coming to this type of event, because it is often held over a meal hour, is that they will be given - or will find - enough food for a meal. If they are not immediately directed to, or cannot find an accessible food source with a sufficient quantity of food without having to stand in a long line, then they will be unhappy. Most planners, and for that matter catering managers, seem unable to get all the parameters right to solve this dilemma, usually because of budget.

- Number of cocktail or dining tables. Another potential disaster waiting to happen. Again, because the expectation of guests is that they will be having a meal, they often load up on their plates from food stations and then cannot find any dining tables at which to sit and eat, or high cocktail tables at which to stand and eat. This is because the planners did not want to spend the money required to get it right and provide sufficient seating for the guests. Remember, it is almost impossible - and certainly very uncomfortable and inconvenient - to have to try to eat a meal from a plate with one hand, hold a drink with the other, and continue to converse at the same time. Even the new plastic wine glass holders that clip onto plates are useless if the drink is a beer!

In calculating the amount of hors d'oeuvres that any single guest will need for this type of event or for any reception-type event, a calculated average will help to alleviate the above problems. For a short, two to three hour reception that is clearly not a meal, an average of four pieces per guest should work. For the larger reception over a meal hour, an average of 10 to 14 pieces per guest should suffice with additional food stations available.

# TABLE STYLES, LAYOUT, SETTINGS, AND DESIGN

Dining tables and table treatments have come a long way in a very short time. Not so many years ago, the only option for guests was round tables and very little in the way of creative table treatment past a standard white tablecloth. There are many more choices today:

## Table Styles

- 60 in. diameter rounds. This table is best suited to eight diners. Optimum spacing between tables is 12 ft, center-to-center or edge-to-edge. This permits adequate space for uncrowded dining and table service. A minimum of 2 ft between opposing chair backs should be allowed.
- 66 in. diameter rounds. This is a compromise table size favored by a few hotels and venues, but it is not as popular as the 60 in. round. It does, however, allow for much more comfortable dining for eight persons. Center-to-center spacing is 12.5 ft when planning table layout.
- 72 in. diameter rounds. This table is one size larger and the seating capacity is nine or ten persons. Optimum center-to-center table spacing is 13 ft, again to permit comfortable seating and safe table service by wait staff.

- Rectangular tables. The normal size for these tables is 8 ft long x 2.5 ft wide. They comfortably seat six guests using a general rule of thumb of approximately 24 in. width x 18 in. depth for each place setting. Less comfortably they can accommodate one more person on each end.
- Octagonal tables. Relatively new, these allow for up to eight persons to sit at the table. A joining bridge section permits two or more of these tables to be joined together, thus giving the potential for very interesting and unusual table arrangements within a room.

## Table Layouts

The distribution of tables throughout the event space is beginning to be explored much more creatively than ever in the past. As mentioned above, optimum table layout design within the event space allows for a minimum of 2 ft between chairs at any two adjacent tables. Furthermore, tables should be optimally placed no closer to walls than 2 ft. This permits safe foot traffic and meal service and is useful in planning room layouts, most often done now on CADD drawings. Frequently, event planners and entertainment producers will bring entertainment right into the audience, which requires much more space in and around tables. Wide aisles and extended stages and dance floors are becoming more common, making the need for detailed floor plans using CADD that much more important.

## Table Settings

By table settings, we are referring to the placement of tableware and glassware at each place. Not everyone is aware of the correct protocol for this placement, although most reputable caterers and hotel catering departments will certainly be knowledgeable. Some items to consider include:

- Allow 24 in. per place setting for adequate space.
- Decide if you want to carry an event theme through all the way to table settings. This can mean of course, special treatment of plates, cups, utensils, and such. For example, a Wild West theme might utilize tin cups, tin plates and a simple steak knife and fork as the only eating utensils. A medieval theme might only use a knife and plate plus a rough wine goblet, with guests expected to use their hands to help them eat the food!
- Decide on the extent of formality to be reflected in the table settings. For example, a country picnic affair with a low budget might only need plastic flatware but the most

formal meal will look best with high quality silverware. Glass stemware for the most formal settings is best.

- Flatware for all courses should be placed at each setting, beginning with the first course always as the outermost setting.
- One glass for each type of beverage or wine served should be provided at each setting.
- Consider using a "charger plate" which is a large service plate pre-set at each place that serves to separate an initial course and a main course without rearranging the setting.
- Remember that not every single place setting or table needs to be exactly the same. Don't be afraid to be creative in settings as long as each guest has the proper flatware and glassware to enjoy the meal. This aspect of table setting is a precursor to the actual overall table design and décor.

## Table Design

Creative table treatment is almost an art in itself. A component of décor, it can be used to carry through the overall event theme, particularly in the color scheme. Table design is also an extension of table settings and the two should be designed together. There are some extremely creative designers out there and they design with some of these considerations in mind:

- Tantalize the senses by incorporating eye-appealing and dramatic table top scenes, sensuous florals for the nose, and different textures in fabrics and linens for touch.
- Coordinate the overall color scheme with proper matching linen in the same or complimentary color families and patterns that may be different but work together.
- Consider the use of chair covers to match or coordinate with the table linens in color and style in order to give a more finished look to the room and the event.
- Try incorporating the menus or event programs into the table design.
- Go for big and dramatic in table centers if budget and sight lines will permit.
- Don't forget to properly illuminate tables and table centers. There are many more choices on the market today than just votive candles, including miniature electric "candles" activated by water, colored miniature electric wire, battery-driven lights of varying colors and duration, and of course external lighting such as ceiling-mounted pin spots. Many of these can actually be incorporated right into the table centers themselves.

# FOOD AND BEVERAGE SELECTION

When choosing a menu, the best advice is to work with a good chef. Often, this will be taken care of for you by the head chef at a venue or hotel. If you are using a catering company, be sure to get several references before making your final choice of company. You want to have the confidence that food quality and creativity are present. Having said that, there is no reason why a little bit of knowledge on the planner's part cannot help to make the meal more exciting. Universally, most chefs will agree on several points:

- Consider a menu that varies textures - crisp vs. smooth, cooked vs. fresh.
- Try varying temperatures - hot soup, cold salad, hot entrée.
- Use taste sensations of varying strengths, generally using stronger tastes later in the meal.
- Consider incorporating local and seasonal dishes.
- Be aware of the growing concern for healthy eating by offering alternative low calorie and low fat foods. Some hotels and caterers now have entire menus devoted to this fare and it is comparable in taste and quality to traditional high fat, high cholesterol diets!
- For wine and other beverage pairing with food courses, be aware of generally what type of wine or drink goes with each course you have chosen and let your chef or sommelier be your guide. The old traditional concept of red wine with red meat and white wine with white meat no longer has to be true. Basically, you should know that the better the pairing, the better will be the effects on people's bodies and digestive systems and hence the more pleasant the dining experience. A simple but nevertheless true example is that of using dessert wines with dessert instead of drinking wine left over from the entrée course with dessert. The excess acidity of the left over wine could not only ruin the taste of the dessert but also cause indigestion.
- Match proper flatware and glassware to the appropriate courses and lay the tables out accordingly. See the earlier section on table layout.
- Remember that an event theme can be carried through even to the food and the way it is presented and served on tables. This can include costumed wait staff, food as décor in table centers or on buffets or other places, and entertainment integrated with food service, or more depending on your imagination.

# OFFSITE CATERING

There will be many instances when events you are planning will not be conveniently held in a hotel. When that happens, you will need to call on the services of an independent caterer who can plan and execute full food and beverage service for your event (although many hotels now have an offsite-catering department). These companies will typically provide a range of services that may include obtaining a liquor license, arranging for tables, chairs, all glassware and flatware, linens, temporary cover such as tenting if the event is outside, and of course all food preparation and service and all beverage service.

When planning an outside-catered event, there are additional considerations compared to a meal at a hotel. Some can be daunting, but not insurmountable, including:

- Is it outdoors or indoors? If outdoors, a whole new set of challenges surfaces. What is the time of day and the time of year? If the event will not be entirely in daylight, then event and meal lighting must be dealt with. This can require tent or other temporary cover and your tent company can provide the right sized tent for the number of people attending.
- If outdoors, lighting will be essential if late in the day. Not only is lighting tables necessary, but also pathways and the entire surrounding area where guests will be walking. Again, temporary lighting can be supplied by most rental equipment companies; however, remember that you must calculate the power requirement for lighting as for stage and decor lighting discussed previously. If there is no appropriate power source for the tenting or the catering close to the event space, then temporary power will need to be brought in.
- If the event is late in the year or in a cooler climate, consider portable radiant heaters for inside the tent, especially in the dining area where guests may get cold while they sit eating. This can happen even on a summer evening. Most such heaters are electric and heat a small area quite comfortably. Propane heaters should not be brought into tents. Larger more permanent heaters are also available that use forced air.
- What is the weather likely to be? If rain is possible, plan accordingly and consider temporary ground cover. There are several companies now that specialize in easily transportable temporary flooring that rolls out to form a nice ground cover that will keep guests dry. Don't forget to keep a pathway for electrical cords for the lighting and cooking power.
- If a full meal is planned, catering will almost always require a food preparation area if

indoors and a separate food preparation tent if outdoors.

- If there are no onsite kitchen facilities, be aware of the need for critical timing in serving a hot meal if one is planned. Don't forget that the food must be prepared in the caterer's kitchen and then brought to the event site in temporary warmers so any delay of service due to speeches or other distractions may result in a less than correctly heated meal. The same comment applies to food that must be served fresh.
- There will be a need for extra staff by the caterer for setup and cleanup of the meal and equipment.
- For setup, ensure that the caterer is aware of all the event details - location, setup time allowed, power, space available.
- Be sure to double check that the catering contract specifies who will be providing the tables, chairs, linens, flatware, and glassware. Not all caterers carry this and you may be responsible for renting it yourself.

Offsite catering and events can be hugely satisfying if for no other reason than the venues and event spaces can be so unusual, thus allowing the event planner some real creative freedom. However, particularly on the catering side, there are many details as outlined that must be covered if the event is to be successful.

Sample Form 15-1: Catering Information Sheet

Date:_____

Day:_____Date:_____Type of Event:_____

Name:_____ Tel:_____

Billing Address:_____

Held At:_____

Address:_____

Contact Person:_____

Phone (W):_____Fax: _____

E-mail: _____

Estimated # of Guests: _____Confirmed By: _____

Time Guests Arrive:_____Type of Bar Service: _____

Tables: _____Types of Wine: _____

Chairs: _____Types of Beer: _____

Size & Color of Linens: _____

Liqueur: _____Champagne: _____

Equip. Available on Site: _____

Mixers: _____Ice: _____

# Bartenders: _____# of Staff: _____

Bar Opens From: _____To: _____

Comments: _____

_____

_____

_____

Deposit: _____ Date Rec'd: _____

Referred by: _____

Table 15-1: Glossary of Catering Terminology

| Term | Description |
| --- | --- |
| **Action Station** | Chefs prepare foods to order and serve them fresh to guests. |
| **à la Broche** | Cooked on a skewer. Also called brochettes, typically beef, chicken, or shrimp. |
| **à la Grècque** | Prepared Greek style with tomatoes, garlic, black olives, and parsley. |
| **à la King** | Cooked in white cream sauce with vegetables (e.g. Chicken a la King). |
| **à la Meunière** | A technique that allows flour to form a thin, golden crust on sautéed or fried items, such as Trout Meunière. |
| **à la minute** | Style of preparation where the food is cooked to order fresh, often right before the guests. Food done a la minute is a perfect suggestion for a food station. |
| **à la Mode** | In the style of: 1. Ice cream on pie 2. Mashed potatoes on beef. |
| **à l' Anglaise** | English style. |
| **à la Provençale** | With garlic and olive oil. |
| **à la Vapeur** | Steamed. |
| **Appellation** | Broadly speaking, the region where a wine is from. When used narrowly, the term signifies the branding offered by wine authorities to indicate the precise origin, grape variety, and heritage of wines. |
| **Apéritif** | A light, pre-dinner alcoholic beverage, often fortified with other flavors, that stimulates the appetite (e.g. Campari, Kirs, and Dubonnet). |
| **Architectural Cuisine** | Menu items that are stacked for height. Also called Vertical Cuisine. |
| **au Gratin** | Foods sprinkled with crumbs and/or cheese and baked until browned. |
| **au Jus** | Served with natural meat juices or gravy without thickening. |
| **au Lait** | Served with milk, as in Café au Lait. |

| | |
|---|---|
| **Bake** | To cook in the oven. Food is cooked slowly with gentle heat, causing the natural moisture to evaporate slowly, concentrating the flavor. |
| **Barbecue** or **Barbeque** | Roasting meat over direct flame or under direct heat similar to broiling, but basted with well-seasoned barbecue sauce. |
| **Blackened** | A popular Cajun-style cooking method in which seasoned foods are cooked over high heat in a super-heated heavy skillet until charred. |
| **Blanch** | To boil briefly to loosen the skin of a fruit or a vegetable. After 30 seconds in boiling water, the fruit or vegetable should be plunged into ice water to stop the cooking action, and then the skin easily slices off. |
| **Boil** | To cook food in heated water or other liquid that is bubbling vigorously. |
| **Braise** | A cooking technique that requires browning meat in oil or other fat and then cooking slowly in liquid. The effect of braising is to tenderize the meat. |
| **Broil** | To cook food directly under the heat source. |
| **Brown** | A quick sautéing, pan/oven broiling, or grilling method done either at the beginning or end of meal preparation, often to enhance flavor, texture, or eye appeal. |
| **Brulé** | Literally "burned," such as with caramelized sugar on crème brulé. |
| **Canapés** | Class of hors d'oeuvre that are always served on small pieces of bread. |
| **Caramelization** | Browning sugar over a flame, with or without the addition of some water to aid the process. The temperature range in which sugar caramelizes is approximately 320° F to 360° F (160° C to 182° C). |
| **Cash Bar** | Guests are charged per drink consumed, before it is consumed, as opposed to an open or hosted bar, where patrons are free to consume, and a final tab is presented to the host for settlement. |
| **Charger** | Another name for a larger plate, used as a base plate or platter. |

| | |
|---|---|
| **Coddle** | A cooking method in which foods (such as eggs) are put in separate containers and placed in a pan of simmering water for slow, gentle cooking. |
| **Confit** | To slowly cook pieces of meat in their own gently rendered fat. |
| **Corkage** | Fee placed on liquor not purchased from the hotel or venue, but either purchased elsewhere, or donated. The fee usually includes the cost of labor, ice, glassware, mixers and occasionally the profit the hotel/venue would have made if you had purchased it from the hotel or venue. |
| **Covers** | Actual number of meals served at a catered meal function or in a restaurant. |
| **Crudités** | A pre-dinner snack, often a raw seasonal vegetable with a dipping sauce, perhaps to accompany an apéritif. |
| **Digestif** | An after-dinner spirited drink that helps to settle the stomach (e.g. Cognac, Jagermeister, Cointreau. |
| **Dessert Parade** | Parade of wait staff all holding desserts, into a dining room, often done with a special dessert such as Baked Alaska. |
| **Dry Snack** | Finger foods, such as nuts, chips and pretzels, often served at receptions. |
| **du Jour** | Of the day. Usually refers to a menu item or specialty for that day. |
| **en Brochette** | Broiled and served on a skewer. |
| **en Casserole** | Food served in the same dish in which it was baked. |
| **en Coquille** | Served in a shell. |
| **en Croûte** | Baked in a flaky crust (e.g. Beef Wellington). |
| **Entrée** | A French term that originally referred to the first course of a meal, served after the soup and before the meat courses. In the United States, it refers to the main dish of a meal. |
| **Flambé** | To ignite a sauce or other liquid so that it flames. |
| **Flute** | To create a decorative scalloped or undulating edge on a piecrust or other pastry. |
| **Fournée** | Baked. |

| | |
|---|---|
| **French Service** | An elegant, complex type of dining service in which entrées are prepared at tableside by wait staff and portioned to patron's plates by the wait staff. Presentation and temperature control become difficult with French service, and accordingly it is used only if the size of the event or venue do not allow plated service or a buffet. |
| **Friandises** | An after dinner treat that could be made with chocolate, marzipan or sugared fruit that accompanies the digestif and coffee. |
| **Fumée** | Smoked. |
| **Ganache** | A rich chocolate filling or coating made with chocolate, vegetable shortening, and possibly heavy cream. It can coat cakes or cookies, and be used as a filling for truffles. |
| **Garnish** | A decorative piece of an edible ingredient such as parsley, lemon wedges, croutons, or chocolate curls placed as a finishing touch to dishes or drinks. |
| **Glaze** | A liquid that gives an item a shiny surface. Examples are fruit jams that have been heated or chocolate thinned with melted vegetable shortening. Also, to cover a food with such a liquid. |
| **Hors d'oeuvres** | Appetizers. |
| **Infusion** | Extracting flavors by soaking them in liquid heated in a covered pan. The term also refers to the liquid resulting from this process. |
| **Julienne** | To cut into long, thin strips. |
| **Jus** | The natural juices released by roasting meats. |
| **Kosher** | Food that is prepared according to Jewish dietary laws. |
| **Marinate** | To combine food with aromatic ingredients to add flavor. |
| **Medallion** | A small round or oval bit of meat. |
| **Mis en Place** | 1. "To put in place" all the preparation for service, including table settings, beverage supplies, china, silverware, etc. |
| | 2. Referring to all the semi-prepared ingredients made ready by the chef before final cooking and presentation. |
| **Napery** | Tablecloths, napkins, and other fabric table coverings. Sometimes also referred to as linens. |
| **Panbroil** | To cook a food in a skillet without added fat, removing any fat as it accumulates. |
| **Panfry** | To cook in a hot pan with a small amount of hot oil, butter, or other fat, turning the food over once or twice. |

| | |
|---|---|
| **Plated Service** | Style of service in which the food is artfully arranged and presented by the chef before the dishes are delivered to the table. It is optimum for temperature control, timing, flavor diversification and presentation, as opposed to a buffet or French service. |
| **Petit Fours** | Bite sized, iced, and elaborately decorated cakes made with any flavor served at the end of a meal. |
| **Preset** | Usually refers to setting in place an appetizer or salad course ahead of guest arrival. |
| **Purée** | To mash or sieve food into a thick liquid. |
| **Roast** | To cook uncovered in the oven. |
| **Roulade** | Rolled, as in meat. |
| **Sans Arête** | Boneless. |
| **Sans Peau** | Skinless. |
| **Sauté** | To cook food quickly in a small amount of oil in a skillet or sauté pan over direct heat. |
| **Scald** | 1. Cooking a liquid such as milk to just below the point of boiling. |
| | 2. To loosen the skin of fruits or vegetables by dipping them in boiling water. |
| **Sear** | Sealing in a meat's juices by cooking it quickly under very high heat. |
| **Season** | To enhance the flavor of foods by adding ingredients such as salt, pepper, oregano, basil, cinnamon, and a variety of other herbs, spices, condiments, and vinegars. Also, to treat a pot or pan (usually cast iron) with a coating of cooking oil and baking it in a 350° F oven for approximately one hour. This process seals any tiny rough spots on the pan's surface that may cause food to stick. |
| **Set** | Let food become solid. |
| **Show Plate** | Decorative plate preset at each place setting during formal meals, which is removed before service begins. |

**Sommelier**   A term that generally refers to someone who is in charge of the cellar, or someone who is considered to be a foremost expert on wines. In Canada, however, the Sommelier Guild certifies wine experts and bestows this prestigious title only after an individual has taken extensive, advanced wine courses and has met stringent requirements. Anyone not having gone through the process should really only be referred to as a "wine steward" or expert.

**Steam**   To cook over boiling water in a covered pan. This method keeps foods' shape, texture, and nutritional value intact better than methods such as boiling.

**Stewing**   Browning small pieces of meat, poultry, or fish, then simmering them with vegetables or other ingredients in enough liquid to cover them, usually in a closed pot on the stove, in the oven, or with a slow cooker.

**Stir-Fry**   The fast frying of small pieces of meat and vegetables over very high heat with continual and rapid stirring.

**Vinaigrette**   A general term referring to any sauce made with vinegar, oil, and seasonings.

**VQA**   Vintner's Quality Assurance. A program run by the Canadian government to guarantee quality and raise awareness for the Canadian wine industry.

# 16

## Other General Resources

**B**esides the most common resources outlined previously, a number of others exist that are used extensively in special events. Each one is a specialty unto itself and the suppliers of these resources can give the planner all the details about the latest technology. Briefly, the other most common ones include:

## TENTING

The specialty of tents has grown immensely over the last 20 years, particularly in special events. The technology is now such that they can be used at almost any time of year. When there is space and budget for a creative and different outdoor environment – or even indoor – tents can be a wonderful departure from the normal indoor event. Here are some of the main concerns when considering the use of tents, with definitions and sketches provided by the Industrial Fabrics Association International:

### Types and Styles

- Pole tents. A tent that features a set of individual poles arranged beneath the fabric roof to support and define the shape of the structure. The fabric roof is tensioned over the poles and attached to ropes and/or cables at designated spots around the fabric's edges. The ropes/cables are anchored to the ground using stakes, augers, or weights around the perimeter of the tent. Pole-supported tents are the grandfather of the tent industry, and were once the only type of tent available. Though they have lost ground to newer designs, pole-supported tents remain popular in the United States and are still considered an important part of most tent rental inventories (Figure 16-1).

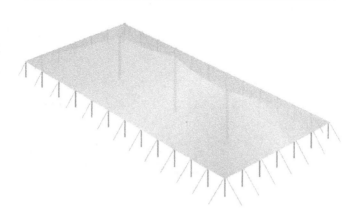

Figure 16-1: Pole Tent Structure

- Pipe frame-supported tents. A tent with an assembled framework made of aluminum or steel pipes that supports the fabric roof and defines the shape of the structure. The rigid framework allows the tent to be freestanding without additional support, but requires the same rope or cable anchoring system as a pole-supported tent to hold it in place, as specified by applicable fire or building codes. Pipe frame-supported tents are popular for events that require smaller tents. Most manufacturers make units as small as 10 ft by 10 ft that are easy to set up and tear down. They are also suitable for smaller events that require few, if any interior obstruction since the frame system makes interior supports unnecessary. Pipe frame-supported tents are available in a wide variety of styles and sizes (Figure 16-2).

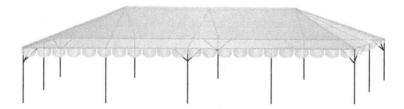

Figure 16-2: Pipe Frame-Supported Structure

- Clearspan tents. A type of tent that features an assembled framework of box beam (or I-beam) arches that support the fabric roof and define the shape of the structure in much the same way as a pipe frame-supported tent. The stronger construction of the aluminum or steelbox-beam frame makes these tents suitable for larger or longer-term applications than other types of tents. The box-beam framework also allows for large areas of unobstructed "clear span" space beneath the fabric roof. The larger structures require heavy equipment because of the size and weight of their parts. Popular in Europe, these tents come in widths ranging from 40 to 200 ft wide.

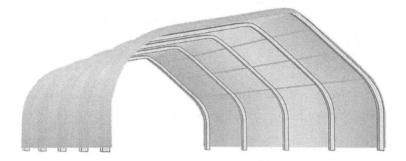

Figure 16-3: Clearspan Tent Structure

- Tensile tent. A type of tent that shares some characteristics with the pole-supported tent, but which relies more on the tensioning of the fabric roof for its structural integrity and shape. The use of tensioned fabric to resist applied loads and shape the fabric membrane means less of a traditional support structure is needed to maintain it. One of the more modern tent designs, tensile tents tend to be more curvilinear and sculpted in appearance than traditional tents. This type of tent can be mass-produced or custom-designed as needed.

Figure 16-4: Tensile Tent Structure

## Fabrics

The primary fabric for tents is vinyl-laminated polyester, but a small percentage of use is still seen for canvas. The newer polyester fabrics are more durable and resistant to weather effects, including water and sunlight damage. All fabrics are treated with flame-retardants.

Most tent sidewalls (pieces of fabric generally attached to the roof structure and used to enclose the sides of tents) are made of lighter weight vinyl-laminated polyester. They – and the roof structure – can be designed with clear vinyl as windows, and can be as large as the entire tent if desired, although with less strength and durability.

## Sizes

Depending on the type of event, here are some general guidelines for determining the size of tent required (also useful for planning indoor events):

- Stand-up reception or cocktail party. 6 ft² per person
- Sit-down dinner. 10 to 12 ft² per person depending on whether the tables seat 10 or 8 persons.
- Buffet table or bar. 100 ft² per 8 ft long table/bar.
- Auditorium or theater-style seating. 6 ft² per person plus 4 to 6 ft width for aisles.
- Dance floor. 2 to 3 ft² per person, assuming 50% of guests dancing at any given time.
- Speaker stage/platform. 10 ft² per person.
- Bandstand. 10 ft² per musician, 20 ft² for drummer, 30 ft² for spinet piano, 100 ft² for full grand piano.

## Setup Considerations

Using tenting successfully does not stop with the choice of type and size of tent. There are many other considerations that need addressing for the event to be successful, including:

- Location. The choice of an appropriate site is essential, and questions to ask include:

    o Is the site large enough to hold the tents and all the activities planned, including stages, tables, chairs, bars, dance floor, catering preparation tent(s), and washrooms?
    o Is the site accessible for trucks of suppliers?
    o Is the ground surface one into which tent anchors can be safely placed?
    o Will tent anchoring disrupt unseen underground infrastructure such as telephone,

gas, water, and hydro?

o How level is the surface and will it present a problem for catering and seating?

- Weather and time of day. The actual date of the event could have a huge effect on setup. Some climates, like British Columbia where I live, are prone to rain, some locales are very dry and hot, some are windy, and some combine all of the above, not to mention varying lengths of daylight at different times of the year. As a result, the planner should know clearly what the likelihood is for any of these conditions to exist during the event and also how much daylight will be available without supplementing lighting. Here are the main areas of concern:

  o Rain. In any potentially wet climate, there must be an allowance made for proper drainage, either by the use of a certain type of tent (some provide better run-off than others), installing sidewalls, or providing portable flooring. Some portable floors are now available which are excellent for this type of event and roll up easily for shipping and installation.

  o Wind. Many tents now can withstand winds of up to 70 mph, such as clearspan tents. If high winds are a possibility during the event, ensure proper anchoring and the proper type of tent.

  o Heat or Cold. This is always a "what if" scenario, like rain. If any doubt at all, one should be prepared for the worst in terms of temperature extremes. If the event will go on after sunset, there is a good chance the temperature may also go down and the tent will need heat. If it is during a hot summer day, it will undoubtedly need air conditioning. Fortunately, there are very good portable propane heaters available for use inside the tent, and also more sturdy, heavier duty air conditioning units and large heaters which are generally mounted outside the tent and blow hot or cold air inside.

  o Darkness. Nothing is worse than finishing dinner inside a tent as the sun sets and you are just ready to begin speeches and dancing, than to realize that the entire environment will soon be in darkness because someone (you?) forgot to check the time of day and lighting needs for the tent. A tent does not come equipped with lights in the ceiling and switches on the walls, so be aware of the need to install portable lamps or some sort of decorative ambient lighting to ensure the space is well illuminated.

- Power. Be absolutely certain exactly what power is required to run the event. Unless you are fortunate to be within a short distance from a building or hydro poles with boxes for 120 V and 208 V electrical tie-in, a portable generator will be needed, most likely for lighting, audio systems, and catering. Many portable power units are now whisper-quiet and can be run continuously for several hours almost undetected. Ensure that you have budgeted for enough fuel and that a tech is readily available if needed in an emergency.

- Human needs and traffic flow. This is an all-too-often neglected area when planning outdoor and tented events. Remember, nothing has been designed for this event until you the planner and your client decided to create it. Therefore, don't forget to consider:

  o Washrooms or portable toilets. Will there be enough and where will they be located? Use the advice of your supplier to determine the number required. If it is a "beer tent," you will obviously need a lot more! Will they be too close to food or dining areas? Is a covered walkway needed to reach them? Is the event long enough that washroom supplies may need to be refilled or toilets emptied? Are there hand cleaner stations available?

  o Traffic flow. I have seen too many situations with tents in which the planner did not anticipate the flow of people during the event. Study the event plan and the tent layout to determine where choke points may occur (washrooms, bars, entrances or exits, around dining tables, around tent structural components, catering prep areas, etc), then adjust your layout accordingly. If you think you may need more space or more tables or an auxiliary tent for something, you most likely will, so don't be afraid to plan for it and price it. It is far better to have more room and more comfort for guests than to have them frustrated by overcrowding.

- Contracts and approvals. Note that in many jurisdictions, particularly within most cities, the city special event department, if there is one, will, by law, require a qualified structural engineer to inspect and certify that your tent setup is structurally sound. You should definitely plan for this, if for no other reason than to avoid potential liability issues. Therefore, allow for sufficient funds to cover this certification and especially allow for time before the event for the engineer to inspect the installation and to give his written blessing.

With respect to contracts for tents, ensure that all details are in the contract. This should include such things as:

o   Extra charges for anchoring.
o   If anchoring in pavement is necessary, will the holes need to be re-filled?
o   Who is delivering what and when?
o   Who is liable for any damage or injuries due to acts of God?
o   Who is responsible for security of the tent equipment if it must remain setup overnight or before or after the event?

With all of these areas covered, you will be well on your way to a successful tented event.

# STAGING

The type and size of special event staging depends on what is happening on the stage, where the stage is located in relation to the audience, and the size of the audience.

If the event is outdoors, the planner must also consider the shape of the ground surface and the weather factor, as well as accessibility to power and other event elements such as changing rooms. Most outdoor staging requires some sort of temporary cover such as special tenting and often, portable power close by. There are now available, easily transportable, fully equipped stages that come as self-contained trucks and include the complete stage surface, trussing for sound and lights, and even some auxiliary power. Most can be erected and ready to go in less than one hour.

There are even temporary support structures that can be used to support staging that covers swimming pools and other previously impossible-to-cover topographical features, so the sky is almost the limit.

If the event is indoors, the planner usually has a choice of using in-house staging such as is found in most hotels and conference centers, or bringing in rented staging from a staging company.

Rectangular staging for special events generally comes in two sizes, 4 ft x 8 ft and 6 ft x 8 ft. Usually, the newer staging systems are expandable in height from 12 in. to 48 in. Invariably, the staging that is found in most venues such as hotels and conference centers is permanently carpeted so if there is a requirement for a hard surface (e.g. tap dancing show) then the choice is either to bring in a wooden-surfaced stage or install a portable wooden dance floor on top of the carpeted stage.

When considering staging for special events, be aware that there are many more choices than just a rectangular stage at the front of the room. If budget permits, consider:

- Using one or more smaller satellite stages for continuous entertainment and action
- Using a center stage for a really impressive show
- Using underlighting and themed stages for effect
- Using different stage heights for more impact
- Using different shapes of stages (may have to be custom built)
- Using a revolve stage (circular, motorized stage that rotates)
- That bands need to be closer to the audience (try a 12 in. or 16 in. high stage, no more) and if possible should be on a separate stage from any other entertainment or event component.

Also be aware that many venues charge separately for staging and it is normally the client's responsibility to cover this expense so you, the planner, will need to ask what it costs in order to keep your client informed.

Along with staging can be included other forms of temporary structural support for events. These include:

- Temporary or roll-up flooring, often used for false floors in tents and in outdoor locations
- Temporary bleachers and seating
- Scaffolding constructed for such things as audio towers for outdoor concert speaker systems.

# SPECIAL EFFECTS

Today's event audiences demand creativity and cutting edge ideas beyond the norm. Special effects (SFX) are probably the most effective way to leave a favorable impression with them and to make them feel they have been treated to something truly spectacular.

Here are some of the currently more common special effects that can be incorporated into almost any event program:

- Fireworks. Refers to larger, slower, higher, longer and bigger, usually outdoors.
- Pyrotechnics. Refers to smaller, more personal, faster, and usually indoors. Can even

be mounted on performers or table centers and remotely triggered.

- Lasers. The old tried and true. The more expensive, usually the more intricate and fancy with customizable designs. Best done in combination with some sort of smoke or haze.
- Smoke and haze. Both are made using different chemical combinations and the planner must be cautious of the effect on guests, the effect on venue sprinkler and smoke alarm systems, and the amount of hang time.
- Fog. Typically created using carbon dioxide ($CO_2$) dry ice in a machine that continuously heats water, or it can be liquid nitrogen based. Used to form a low-lying layer of fog on the floor or on a stage. Be wary of drafts causing it to dissipate too fast.
- Snow. Can be created from different chemical combinations that either stay on a surface or melt immediately. Snow machines used in the movie industry now have the capability to provide continuous indoor storms over a fairly wide area.
- Water and rain. Can use "dancing waters", fountains, movie rain sprinkler systems, or the latest water scrims that can be used as stage backdrops to reflect video or lights, or can be parted to let people or other things through without getting wet.
- Streamers and confetti. Come as "cannons" in various sizes and can be hand-held or remotely triggered. Streamers can now be customized with corporate logos. Be careful of the material they are made from because some are not waterproof and can also cause stains if wet.
- Fire. Spectacular and can be hand-held or used in choreography. Be extremely cognizant of safety and venue fire regulations.

For all special effects, the planner must continuously be aware of and plan for, safety and the effect on human beings, including evacuation of people and the quickest possible evacuation of chemicals from the atmosphere. Note the "Word of Caution" below under Risk Management that event insurance for high-risk activities is increasingly difficult to obtain, meaning anything out of the ordinary that involves fire and/or indoor pyrotechnics.

Lastly, remember that SFX should be used sparingly but effectively, and should build to a climax.

# TRANSPORTATION

Occasionally, an event planner will have to provide transportation to, from, or within an event. This is yet another area where creativity and theming can be used. Here are some ideas to consider for transportation:

- Try a parade of classic cars to transport guests.
- Try adding specialized entertainment as guests are boarding transportation to keep them occupied and add to a theme.
- Place entertainers on the buses or transportation to interact with guests.
- Create unusual situations during a trip such as pirates boarding a cruise boat or outlaws holding up an excursion train.
- Use limousines for transporting guests on a scavenger hunt or quest-type game.
- Use helicopters and airplanes for special sightseeing or a grand entrance to impress VIPs.
- Bring transport right into the event space, such as driving an old "woody" into a beach party themed event.
- Use transportation for group photo opportunities.
- Take guests for day-long adventures on horseback, snowmobiles, kayaks, classy yachts, off-road vehicles, dune buggies, and tie the experience in to a conference or event theme.

As you can see, there are endless possibilities, with lots of specialties, depending on the location of the event.

Keep in mind the requirement for proper coordination of transportation. At the very minimum, you will need a coordinator at each end of a transportation route, and possibly more than one if the total number of guests to be transported is large. Radios and/or cell phones are useful to keep in contact with each other in order to prepare for arrivals and departures and to bring buses or other vehicles to the embarkation/disembarkation point with minimal waiting and possible traffic congestion.

Don't forget to coordinate with all appropriate organizations involved to ensure you have permission to operate and/or park the transportation in a given area. For most cities, special permission will need to be obtained well in advance and temporary "No Parking" signs erected in the transportation pickup and drop-off area. Normally, the lost parking revenue will have to be reimbursed to the city.

Frequently, transportation companies have minimum call times for their vehicles, such as four hours, and you will be charged for the driver's time regardless of whether the time of your event is less than this amount. Also, allow for the time to and from the vehicle garage within the total time quoted.

Finally, most transportation companies do not include any gratuities in their quotes although one is typically expected for all drivers at the end of their shift with you, so ensure that it is also part of your budget.

## PUBLIC RELATIONS, PRINTING, ARTWORK AND SPECIALTY ITEMS

For theming, don't forget that a theme can be augmented with any type of written or unique material including invitations, menus, event programs, items of clothing, gifts, advertising, special notices, and thank-you cards. The more coordinated and used the theme, the more effective will be the response to your planning and ideas.

In the case of larger events, typically festivals and public events, public relations is a continuing method of reinforcing the theme and message of the event to the point that potential attendees come to associate the theme with the event. For example, repeated radio, TV, and billboard advertising, programming in newspapers, media interviews, and public appearances can be themed and structured to reinforce the image of the event. This is most useful for fundraisers and public events.

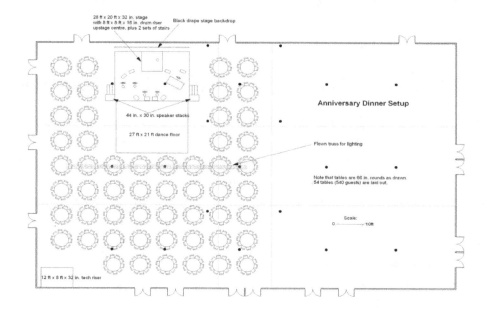

Plate 1: Example of 2-D CADD: Simple Event Floor Plan
Courtesy Pacific Show Productions

Plate 2: Example of 3-D CADD
Design courtesy Peter Neufeld Design, Sydney, Australia

Plate 3: Example of Large Décor Props: A False-Fronted Western Street
Courtesy Wayne Chose & Associates Photography and Pacific Show Productions

Plate 4: Example of Fabric and Floral Décor: Table Linens and Centerpieces
Courtesy Pacific Show Productions

Plate 5: Example of Octagonal Dining Table Layout
Courtesy Event Solutions Magazine, MH Concepts, and Visual WOW

Plate 6: Example of A-V as Part of a Stage Set
Courtesy Pacific Show Productions

Plate 7: Interactive Entertainment Always Works
Courtesy Vision Masters Photography and Pacific Show Productions

Plate 8: Example of Special Effects: Indoor Fire Choreography
Courtesy Wayne Chose & Associates Photography and Pacific Show Productions

# Part Five

# Event Evolution:
# The Coordination and
# Execution Phases

# 17

## Risk Management

### PART ONE: IN THE EVENT COORDINATION PHASE

The following comments on risk management are a combination of personal experience and the insight of three experts, Dr. Joe Jeff Goldblatt[6], Barbara Dunn[7], and Bill Knight[8].

What exactly is risk as it pertains to special events? By definition it can be considered as any condition or occurrence that might affect the outcome of an event. It includes everything that can happen financially, legally or ethically. Risk management is a very important area of concern in professional event management and planning, and obviously, in larger events requires a thorough examination and analysis, as it can be quite costly. In smaller events, it is not quite as likely to incur high costs, especially if the event is private, but it nevertheless requires careful consideration.

Risk management analysis is essentially a process that consists of five steps:

### Identifying the Risks

Use staff and suppliers to assist with this. Keep a detailed list of the risks. Prepare appropriate plans to reduce or deal with these risks accordingly.

### Measuring the Risks

Identify the most serious and the ones most likely to recur then prioritize your list according to the most severe.

### Controlling the Risks

This consists of four generally accepted techniques:

- Risk avoidance. This means don't do it at all. Either don't take the risk or totally eliminate it. For example, don't serve alcohol.

- Risk reduction. If you must live with the risk as part of the event, minimize its impact on you and the event and control your potential losses. This is best done by a thorough analysis and understanding of the potential risk and the consequences. For example, add handrails to stage stairs to minimize the risk of people falling.

- Risk retention. Accept certain responsibility for the risk, and ensure that all concerned players are educated about the risk. For example, you may be partially responsible for damages caused by your suppliers, so have proper and adequate insurance.

- Risk transfer. Try to transfer the risk to other persons or organizations. For example, if you have a physical activity for guests, ensure they sign a waiver.

## Putting Controls into Effect

What are some of the more common potential sources of liability for a typical event, how do they relate to the list above, and how are they handled by the event planner? These are some of the main ones:

- Liquor liability. This is typically the host's responsibility so you as the planner must ensure that the host (normally the client) has obtained the necessary training for servers (e.g. "Serving it Right" course). This is an example in which there is always the option of risk avoidance by not serving alcohol, or at least by providing free transportation.

- Copyright and licensing. This pertains primarily to the copyright of music but can also extend to the area of recording live performances by any means, either video or audio. The organizations responsible for distributing and collecting fees are ASCAP (American Society of Composers, Authors & Publishers) in the USA and SOCAN (Society of Composers, Authors, and Music Publishers of Canada) in Canada, for music. The obligation for paying the fees to these organizations usually falls to the venue. However, in the case of taping performances, performers and their respective unions should be asked for permission (e.g. ACTRA, EQUITY, SAG, AFTRA and others), and all details should be spelled out clearly in contracts.

- Permits and licenses. Generally speaking, the larger the event, the higher the probability of requirements for permits and licenses to carry out certain activities. The event planner must be in a position to know where and when to obtain these permits and licenses and how much they cost so they can be included in the event budget. They originate from a variety of sources, including municipal, provincial/state, federal, and private. Table 17-1 is a list of the more common requirements. Note that many of these would only pertain to large outdoor, public events:

Table 17-1: Typical Sources for Permits and Licenses

| Permit/License | Source |
| --- | --- |
| Alcohol | Provincial (State) Liquor Licensing Branch |
| Bingo, Lottery and Gaming | Provincial (State) Gaming Department |
| Business | Municipal government |
| Electrical tie-in | Hydro company and Municipal government |
| Employee and volunteer health insurance | Workers Compensation Board |
| Food handling | Municipal Health Department |
| Music | SOCAN (Canada), ASCAP (USA) |
| Occupancy | Fire Department |
| Parades | Municipal government and Police |
| Parking and Street Closures | Municipal government and Police |
| Parks Usage | Parks Department or Board |
| Public Assembly | Municipal government and Police |
| Fireworks and Pyrotechnics | Fire Department |
| Sales Tax | Provincial (State) and federal revenue departments |
| Signs and Banners | Municipal Zoning Department |
| Temporary Structures (e.g. scaffold towers, staging, tenting) | Stress analysis by professional engineer and approval by municipal government |

- Recreational activities. For many events these days, there is more and more emphasis on participation, much of it done in the interest of teambuilding. Frequently, these activities involve some element of risk, especially physical injury. Examples might include certain rides and simulator games, rock climbing, canoeing, horseback riding, skiing, and many more. The prudent event planner must ensure that the risk in these cases is transferred to the participant by means of a release or waiver that must be signed by each participant individually. A second method - and one that should be only supplementary - is to have the client name the planner and all participants as "additional insured" on their blanket liability insurance policy.
- Regular event activities and insurance. This is a catch-all category that I personally

include to cover such diverse areas as:

o Personal injuries to, or caused by, performers and suppliers (e.g. a guest is injured by indoor pyrotechnics)
o Personal injuries to, or caused by, guests or attendees (e.g. a guest trips a performer during a routine in which the performer roams amongst tables. and the performer breaks a leg)
o Property loss or damage caused by performers and suppliers (e.g. a decorator damages a venue wall when hanging props)
o Property loss or damage caused by guests and attendees (e.g. guests steal a number of expensive table centers).

Essentially, these are all risks that the planner must live with. Otherwise, there would never be any event at all. They are primarily safety issues and form the biggest single area of concern for the event planner, as each event is different. It is in this area that all personnel must be particularly vigilant before, during, and after the event in order to prevent any of these from happening. The most common method of protection, besides a thoroughly safety-conscious attitude amongst all event stakeholders, is property and liability insurance. Most event companies now carry a minimum of $1 million and ideally up to $5 million of liability insurance. Property insurance can often be available on a temporary basis only, especially if some of the equipment or property of concern has an inordinately high value (e.g. an art exhibition), and will also cover property in transit. Event planners should consult an insurance company with experience in event insurance for these types of insurance. In some cases, such as property loss or damage caused by guests, a clause can be inserted in contracts to protect loss.

**A Word of Caution.** In the post 9/11 world and post Rhode Island night club fire world, insurance companies have been loathe to insure event planning companies for what they deem to be a relatively high-risk business. This has led to exorbitant increases in annual insurance premiums for event planners, not to mention a new requirement now almost universal, that all participating members of an event team must cross-insure each other (i.e. to name each other on their own policies as "additional insureds"). It has also led to the virtual disappearance of liability insurance for any sort of pyrotechnics whatsoever. Although we hope that this will not be permanent, it has definitely led to less emphasis on "pushing the envelope" in terms of high-risk effects and activities for at least the near future.

- Security. For most small private events, security is not of concern. Even with larger events in convention centers or hotels, the regular venue security staff is usually sufficient to prevent any loss or injury. This changes when valuable equipment or personal goods may have to be left overnight in a room that would not normally have adequate security for proper protection. In these cases, additional staff may need to be hired in order to keep insurance policies valid. Who pays for this security must be established at the outset prior to the event and prior to a contract being in place.

  For larger public events, security is a much more complex issue and may involve the hiring of a private security company in addition to a police presence. In this case, a planner should set up a full security plan, taking into account such variables as:

  o Whether liquor will be available or served. Yes means more security personnel.
  o Number of attendees. A higher number means more security personnel.
  o Ages of attendees. If in the early twenties, more security personnel will be needed.
  o Type of event. A rock concert will mean more security personnel than a family event.
  o Time of event. Late night usually means more security personnel.
  o Ease of dispersal after event or even ease of entry before event. The more difficult and slow either of these is, the more security personnel will be needed.
  o Number of access points. More means more security personnel.

  Only after a thorough assessment of all these and other factors can a good decision be made about the number, qualifications and cost of security.

- Disasters, crises, and acts of God. Some of these might include:

  o Flooding
  o Destruction of property by fire
  o Terrorism
  o Food poisoning
  o Power outages
  o Celebrity talent cancellation
  o Strikes
  o Flight cancellations

o    Bankruptcy of client, venue, or major supplier.

For most of these, a planner must consider the ramifications; however, there are only certain remedies that can be dealt with ahead of time, the main one being to include contract clauses transferring liability if one or more does occur, and clauses allowing for an alternative means of dealing with the problem and still holding the event, such as alternate locations or alternate performers. The main point is that the planner should be aware that these can happen and should know who and when to contact when they do.

# PART TWO: IN THE EVENT EXECUTION PHASE

## Monitoring Risk

The primary focus of risk management during the event execution phase is the fifth risk management step, that of actually monitoring the risk. By now you will have in place all the necessary insurance, all necessary licenses, all waivers, all security, all personnel training, and any other approvals and protection needed. However, you and your team must remain ever vigilant so that your safeguards are not put to the test. How is this done and what do you look out for? During the event execution phase, risk management is directed towards the site itself and any potential hazards. See Sample Form 20-1 at the end of Chapter 20 for a comprehensive checklist for the event day(s) and setup/strike day(s).

# 18

## Personnel Management

### PART ONE: IN THE EVENT COORDINATION PHASE

Event planning is more than anything a "people" business. If you dislike working with people and taking the good with the bad, then it's the wrong business for you. If however, you are like the vast majority of event planners and thrive on the adrenalin rush of leading an enthusiastic team to create an unbelievable event experience, then you are in the right place.

Your first real taste of personnel or human resources management comes in the event coordination phase. Here are some general guidelines for working with paid staff/subcontractors and volunteers in this part of the process.

### Assembling the Team

Assuming for the time being that most of your team will be subcontractors, then here are some tips to consider:

- Call all suppliers and confirm names of personnel who will be working on the event.
- Re-confirm all contract details with suppliers.
- Review all scheduling with suppliers.
- Ensure all event stakeholders (including the venue, all suppliers, and other people involved who may not be subcontracted by you such as caterers or an A-V company) have the same event details you have (e.g. date, location, setup schedule, etc.).
- Search for and hire extra help as required, such as stage managers.
- Outline all duties for subcontractors and extra help.

## Working with the Team

This is where leadership and good management come in. Here are some tips:

- Determine your leadership style (which you should know intimately anyway!). Don't forget that many people in the industry, especially suppliers and performers, are very independent and may not respond well to an autocratic style, but more to a democratic style. Bear in mind that in the end, it is your event and you must live with all decisions.

- Delegate as much as possible, even to suppliers. Just be sure that along with the delegation you also transfer the responsibility for the job and more importantly, the authority to make the necessary decisions.

- Let everyone know the reporting hierarchy for the event, including where you, the suppliers, the team, and the client all fit in.

- Ensure that the entire team has as much information as possible about the event: who it is for, the background of the client, how they all fit in to the scheme, the time, date, location, load-in details, strike details, and hours of work.

- Badges and attire. Ensure that the team knows the standard of dress and whether they must wear badges or other clothing identifying them as part of the team or are able to wear their own company attire.

- Provide basic amenities. Understand that people cannot go forever without a break. Allow for crew meal breaks and if possible, provide and budget for at least basic sandwiches and soft drinks.

- Ensure that the event team will have safety wear as required by Workers Compensation Board (WCB).

## Working with Volunteers

In many large public events such as festivals, volunteers are one of the most important and often sole means of staffing. Some important points to consider when working with volunteers are:

- Recruiting and selection. Try to write enticing and attractive ads and place them in as many locations as possible. Ensure contact information is clear and when they apply, ensure that there is a method on the application form to determine their talents through selective questions. Don't forget to determine when is the best time for them to work as it relates to your event and don't forget to let them know about all the important details, including incentives like free parking, food, free concerts or attendance, amenities like free clothing, and of course, event details.

- Orientation. An orientation meeting for all volunteers prior to the event is essential to "turn them on" and generate enthusiasm. At the meeting, be sure to outline all the benefits and recognition of volunteering as above, ensure they are given schedules of when, where and for whom they will be working, outline all the details of the event, double check to ensure they are working in the areas they most want to and are qualified to, and provide training to those who might need it.

- Volunteer handbook. If the event is complicated, it is well worth the effort to compile a volunteer handbook that outlines all the details of the event, including time, date, location, maps and site/floor plans, specific volunteer duties and shifts, parking information, names and contact numbers, and any other useful information.

- Motivation. Also keep in mind that volunteers are sometimes not as motivated as contracted personnel. Therefore, due to no-shows and the fact that you cannot demand work from them, you will undoubtedly require more volunteers to do a job than a contractor would need to do the same job. It's just a fact of human nature.

- Most importantly, keep in mind that volunteers do so for many reasons: a sense of community service, personal achievement, as a hobby to collect recognition amenities, and others. More than anything, they want to know that they are appreciated, so whatever you do, make that the continuing emphasis.

# PART TWO: IN THE EVENT EXECUTION PHASE

Once onsite, your whole job is devoted to directing your event team. It is entirely personnel management. You must know your team, what they are capable of, and what you need to accomplish with them. Here are some considerations:

- Ensure the entire team is aware of the goal of the event, what must be set up, the schedule for setup and strike, and the event running order.
- Ensure the team knows the floor or site plan intimately and understands where their component fits in.
- Liaise with the various members of your team and venue staff to minimize conflicting tasks.
- Ensure the team has appropriate attire, including identifying clothing and appropriate safety gear (e.g. steel-toed boots, hard hats if rigging, etc).

- Ensure personnel operating specialty equipment such as genie lifts or electrical hookup, are properly qualified.
- Plan for crew breaks and try to fit them around other tasks that are best done without that particular component of your team in order to minimize downtime.
- Consider working conditions and watch for hazards such as too much noise, wet or cold weather, slippery surfaces, fire or electrical hazards, and give breaks or shelter as needed. Ensure that first aid is easily accessible.
- Allow sufficient time to brief your team well before each major segment of the event (e.g. a briefing before tech setup, a briefing before rehearsals and sound checks, a briefing before the event, and a briefing before strike).
- Conflict resolution. Deal with conflicts as soon as they occur. Don't let them simmer. Usually, the event environment is so temporary that it is better to try to separate conflicting parties for the duration, but each case must be weighed on its own merits.
- Have emergency contact information for all key personnel.

Our company uses a comprehensive rider for all supplier contracts that addresses reporting procedures, attire, and other issues so that there is no confusion when they get onsite. This rider was created based on our experience and is used to minimize any potential problems with the various different suppliers at an event site. It is attached as Sample Form 19-5 at the end of Chapter 19: Contract Management.

# 19

# Contract Management

Where would we be without contracts? One would like to think that we would be a less litigious society but who is going to be the first one to test the theory? Unfortunately, nobody in the special event industry, so we continue having to write down everything we plan to do and even make plans for things we do not even want to do. This is what forms the basis of contracts and an event planner must be very knowledgeable in this area or at least know the basics and where to go to get help. Hopefully, this section will act as a primer. It is based on personal experience combined with some good words from a number of other experts and colleagues in the industry. Contract law is a complex topic, so please note that this is not intended as a substitute for legal advice. In fact, it is highly recommended that event planners seek competent advice before drawing up any form contracts for their business.

For the most part, event planners will work with two types of contracts, those between the planner and the client, and those between the planner and suppliers. If you are serious about your business, it behooves you to create two different form contracts for each of these types, preferably with your own company letterhead. However, before you do, it is useful to know exactly what you are getting into. Much of the following information is excerpted from a presentation by Sheryl Daly at Pacific Contact 2001 sponsored by the British Columbia Touring Council for the Performing Arts[10], with some added comments from Terry Quick of ENTCO International in Seattle[11]. It includes four main components:

- What is a contract?
- What to include in a contract
- Signing and issuing contracts
- Breaking a contract.

# WHAT IS A CONTRACT?

A contract in our industry is a bilateral agreement. In other words, it is between two or more people or parties. It explains an obligation in which each party mutually acquires a right to what is promised by the other. More than anything, it is a tool that outlines the details of an agreement. Most importantly, it is legally binding.

A contract should always be in writing and should:

- Use clear words and uncluttered language
- Represent and protect mutual interests
- Spell out the details of an agreement
- Withstand scrutiny in the legal sense.

Why in writing? Because a verbal or oral contract is too confusing and is hard to enforce if there is a dispute. It is far too easy for the two sides to have different recollections of what each promised to the other.

The key elements of a binding contract are:

## Competent Parties

Each side must have the capacity to enter. For example, minors cannot enter into a contract without parental consent and anyone under the influence of alcohol or drugs or deemed mentally incompetent at the time of signing is not competent.

## Consideration

If one party is to be held to the contract, there must be something given in exchange, normally money (or possibly property or rights).

## Meeting of the Minds

This means "mutual assent." Both sides must be clear about the details, rights, and obligations of the contract.

# WHAT TO INCLUDE IN A CONTRACT

There are two main parts to contracts, Terms and Conditions, and Clauses.

## Terms and Conditions

These are what can be considered the variable parts of a contract, those myriad details pertaining to this specific event. They would include such information as:

- Contact Information (pertains to client and supplier contracts):

  o Legal name of client and planner organizations (or individual), and in the case of suppliers and artists, their stage name or company or individual names
  o Contact person(s) with signing authority
  o Mailing address
  o Physical address
  o Phone/fax number
  o E-mail address.

- Event Details (pertains to client and supplier contracts):

  o Event venue name, specific room name if applicable, address, phone number, contact person, date, start and end times of event, start time/setup/strike times for suppliers and artists, technical and rehearsal times, length of performance if entertainment show.
  o Specifics of service(s) or product(s) to be provided in detail, including a list of all components (e.g. lighting or audio detailed list, list of décor items and where and how they will be used, etc), number of persons involved if applicable (e.g. number of performers in an act for a supplier/artist contract).
  o Specifics of additional services to be provided by either the client in the case of client/planner contracts or by the planner in the case of planner/supplier contracts. For example, the client may be asked to provide the audio system, or a changing room, or food and beverages for staff. In the case of extras the planner may have to provide for suppliers, the same may apply only if it is "passed down the line" to the planner.

- Financial Information:

  o Compensation for services/products provided.
  o Taxes as applicable. Note that in Canada the 6% GST (goods and services tax)

is payable across the country on event services contracts. For some items other sales taxes (provincial/state) are payable and are very specific to the province or state so ensure that you have all the correct details in writing from the appropriate provincial or state authorities. A tax audit is not pretty and can cause instant bankruptcy if you have not done your homework.

   o   Deposit amounts and deadlines. Common practice amongst most event companies now seems to be a deposit of 50 to 75% upon contract signing with the remainder due on or before the actual event.

- Rider Information. Often in cases of celebrity talent or other specialized suppliers, there is a "rider" that forms part of their contract. This rider can include many additional requirements to the main contract and in some cases the cost of the rider may approach the cost of the basic contracted services! It may include such things as transportation and accommodation requirements (e.g. first class airfare for "x" persons from Toronto, first class single, non-smoking hotel rooms, etc), food and meal requirements, green room (changing room) requirements, and technical specifics (e.g. stage plot, audio and lighting requirements, and/or backline equipment such as extra instruments, amplifiers, etc). We often try to negotiate out of "silly" requirements that are not needed (e.g. 20-year old Scotch, yellow jelly beans, etc) and this is where a skilled entertainment agent or producer can help navigate the tricky waters of celebrity talent. The rider will come with the supplier contract and should in turn be passed on to, or made part of, the planner/client contract.

## Clauses

These are what may be referred to as the "boiler plate" or fixed part of the contract. They generally do not vary from one event to the next and may include such items as:

- Cancellation policy. Details how much is payable to the planner or to the supplier in the case of a cancellation by the client or planner respectively (basically the client in either case does the canceling). Most event companies nowadays seem to enforce a policy that entitles them to full payment if the event is cancelled within 14 days of the event date, with a sliding scale of decreasing penalties going back from that date.
- Termination policy. Indicates what will happen if either party fails to perform any or all of its respective obligations. This may include the amounts payable to the parties and the amount of time and method required to indicate termination (e.g. must give

30 days notice in writing).

- Force majeure. Removes liability from one or more of the parties due to unavoidable circumstances preventing them from performing their obligations, such as an act of God (e.g. snowstorm), strikes, natural disasters, or failures of third parties. Sometimes it may allow for substitutions to be made.

- Legal jurisdiction. Names the province/state and municipality in which the governing law and legal cases are to be heard and dealt with.

- Arbitration. Outlines arbitration or possible "alternate dispute resolution" as the preferred method for solving disputes instead of litigation.

- Intellectual property. Particularly in the case of planner/artist contracts, this outlines any restrictions on the recording of performances.

- Performing organizations and unions. Indicates that the contract is subject to regulations of performing or trade unions.

- Rights of assignment. Prevents either party from selling their interest to a third party without mutual consent.

- Independent contractor status. Specifies that the contractor is an independent contractor and therefore responsible for all income tax and Workers Compensation Board deductions.

- Other. Often useful for certain event contracts, this specifies what is and what is not normally payable on a regular basis and as a matter of course. For example, we include a clause that says that electrical hookup fees, staging, and copyright license fees are normally payable by the client. Likewise, we remind them that all props or equipment, unless otherwise stated in the terms of the contract, are considered rentals and any loss or damage may be billed to the client at replacement cost.

Following this chapter are several samples of contracts between an event planner - or producer - and a client, and between an event planner and a supplier. Note that some are more complex than others. That does not necessarily mean that they are not as "tight." In the case of our company, we prefer to treat each event with a little more flexibility and to incorporate more specific terms for each one regarding some of the items above that one might normally consider as clauses. Our experience has shown that simplicity seems to work the best (i.e. it assumes honesty to start, rather than emphasizing a fear of litigation), but that is not necessarily the same experience as others. You as a planner will have to decide how much you want to try to "tie up" your clients and suppliers on paper.

# ISSUING AND SIGNING CONTRACTS

## Software

A quick word about the actual "physical creation" of the contract before going into issuing. Our experience has determined that it is best to use some sort of electronic contract if possible in order to save time. As a planner, you will be writing many contracts over the course of your career, and the task is made much easier by using a relational database program such as Microsoft Access or one of the excellent event planning software suites available on the market. Basically, such a program enables you to incorporate many individual databases (e.g. in our case these are clients, suppliers, and venues) and to create forms and reports (e.g. contracts) that integrate all of them. Thus, with some customization, they can be made to create all the contracts you will need for any event by entering the data only once. The added benefit is that for repeat clients, suppliers, or venues, only the specifics of that particular event need be entered and the software does the rest of the work, including providing you with as many statistics and reports as you will need. Note the sample contracts at the end of this chapter.

## Issuing Contracts

There are several points to be clear on here, even though issuing a contract seems to be straightforward:

- Always include a deadline date to receive the contract back.
- Send at least two signed copies to the other party along with any riders.
- If both parties (e.g. you and a supplier) want to issue their own contracts, this creates what lawyers call the "battle of the forms," and you should be wary. Check the other person's contract to ensure that there are no contradictory clauses or statements. If there are, try to agree on whose interpretation is correct and put it in writing and/or change the offending contract and initial the change. Note that legally, any changes must be initialed by both parties to the contract.
- According to the "mailbox rule," a signed contract that is mailed is effective the moment it is deposited in a mailbox.
- Faxed contracts are generally acceptable but to be on the safe side, try to get a hard copy mailed to you.
- Always keep a hard copy of the signed contract on file.
- Note that all items on a contract are negotiable before and until the contract is signed by both parties.

- If there are any changes, it is always best to re-issue a revised contract that includes the revision date, but if you cannot, ensure changes are authorized in writing by your client or accepted by your supplier in writing.

## Signing a Contract

Here are some tips to consider before signing, although this is a generally straightforward component of contract law:

- Double check all event details and ensure names are spelled correctly.
- Always date your own signature and leave room for a date for the other party.
- Ensure that the other party has signing authority. It's better to know ahead of the event if the client representative signing the contract is the same person issuing the check or if will you have to chase someone totally unknown to you. Try to have the same person who signs the contract also be responsible for signing your check.
- If you are signing a supplier's contract rather than your own, again re-check all details to ensure that they agree with what you are contracting the supplier for. If they don't, then make the necessary changes in ink and initial them. Insist that the supplier also sign at your initials and send back to you a copy of the revised contract.

## Breaking a Contract

A broken contract is one of those situations that a planner dreads; however, if you are going to be in business for yourself, there will be instances when it will happen. Unfortunately, it is a part of business and a part of human nature. You should have some idea of what your remedies are, whether it is you or your client who has committed the breach.

When does a breach occur? These are the main ways:

- When one party fails to stick to his part of the agreement. (e.g. Your client does not pay you the required deposit on time, thus also making it impossible for you to pay a deposit to your celebrity talent who subsequently cancels.)
- When one party makes it impossible for the other to perform. (e.g. Your client guaranteed that the venue would be available for five hours for setup after their afternoon meeting, but ended up going overtime and only allowed you two hours. You have to completely drape the room in black curtains but cannot do so in the given time.)
- When a party to the contract does something against the intent of the contract. (e.g. Your absolutely fabulous comedy magician was supposed to deliver a family show but

instead added his own color in the form of "blue" material, thus forcing mothers to cover their children's ears!)

- When a party absolutely refuses to perform the contract. (e.g. Your very experienced but somewhat irrational A-V producer states that he will not run your show unless you retract the comments about his mother wearing army boots.)

What do you do? For the event planner, a contract breach can spell potential disaster, especially if it is close to or possibly at, the event. In these cases, here are some tips:

- Be firm about the contract terms and details, but remain willing to communicate.
- Remind the offending party of the agreement but be as calm as possible and try to work out differences in a rational manner.
- Consider alternative solutions that may solve the problem in order to buy time until the event is over.
- Try to get a third neutral party involved to assist.

If the breach occurs at a non-critical time in relation to the execution of the event or if the differences between the parties are such that the event can still proceed at least under a slightly modified agreement, then following the event try to ensure that all differences and specifics are immediately conveyed in writing between the offending parties.

## Resolving Disputes

If, after everything has been tried and all details of differences have been recorded, there are several methods to use to settle disputes:

- Alternative dispute resolution (ADR). This is simply the use of mediation or arbitration to solve the dispute. It can be written into your standard contracts as a clause so that once the contract is signed, both parties are bound by it as the favored method of resolving disputes. ADR can significantly reduce the costs of a lawyer and a long, costly legal battle and should be seriously considered as a contract clause.
- Small claims court. In most jurisdictions, these are typically used to recover disputed amounts that are under $10,000 or sometimes more. They are quite simple to work in and an individual company owner or event planner can easily go through the process without a lawyer, although some professional help is always wise. Keep in mind two things, however. First, the process can be very lengthy and can take over a year just

to get to court, mainly because of the backlog of court cases. Second, even if you win in court, there is no guarantee that you will be paid and the hardest part often comes after the court judgment in trying to collect on the judgment.

- Lawsuit. This assumes that the disputed amount is over $10,000 (or the top limit of small claims court). This is to be avoided at all costs. If it happens, you will need expert legal advice and probably very deep pockets.

Thus, the best way to settle breaches of contract is between the two parties directly with each one being willing to see the other's point of view. A little humility never hurt anyone and in the case of an event planner looking to establish a reputation, it just may help to save that reputation. That being said, if the breach involves only the lack of payment of the contract amount or part of it and all other services have been delivered as required, then the best defense is a continued, polite attack on accounts receivable.

Once all the contracts have been issued and signed and the required deposits have been received, if you have done your job properly, all you need to do now is wait until the event date approaches and then you swing into action again with the next phase, Event Execution.

# SAMPLE CONTRACTS

At the end of this chapter are several sample contracts, including two samples of client contracts and two samples of supplier contracts. The reader is welcome to use these to form the basis of her own contracts; however, again remember that these sample contracts should not be used without first obtaining the advice of a lawyer experienced in contract law, specifically within the jurisdiction of the planner.

In Sample Form 19-1, the Simple Client Contract, this contract contains a minimum number of clauses, and even those that have been included are very simple. Specific details of each event are normally completed either on the contract itself or as a rider if space is insufficient on the main page of the contract.

In Sample Form 19-2, the Medium Complex Client Contract, the main body of the contract contains all the clauses, and the details of every event are specified on a rider. This type of contract more strictly binds the client.

In addition, there is a sample rider to a supplier contract that outlines some general requirements for suppliers. It has been based on a similar form for suppliers who work with our company. It may be used or modified for the reader's own purposes.

Sample Form 19-1: Simple Client Contract

## MEMORANDUM OF AGREEMENT

Production No: 02120503                     Producer: Arthur Fancypants

THIS AGREEMLENT made and entered into on this date,     April 15, 2003     by and between:

(Organization): XYZ Insurance Co.

by (Contact):    Joan Getalife

hereinafter called the CLIENT, and ABC Event Company Ltd., as Producer.

The Producer agrees to present the following:

> 7:00 - 9:00pm - Background music by the Musical Marvels jazz ensemble
> 9:00 - 10:00pm - Stage show by the Fabulous Friars comedy troupe
> All audio and lighting to be included. Setup and sound check at 5:00pm.

At: Best Sleep Hotel                        On:  December 5, 2003
5490 West Honeysuckle St.
New Orleans, BC                             Time of Show(s): 7:00 PM

In: Pinnacle Ballroom                       Length of Show: 1 hour

For this program, I/We the undersigned agree to pay ABC Event Company Ltd. the sum of:

$10,000.00 plus  $0.00 PST plus  $700.00 GST  = $10,700.00 (GST Reg.#R123904997)

**Advance due with return of signed Agreement Memo:**        **$7500.00**

1.    TERMS: 75% of contract value due with return of signed Agreement Memo within 14 days of receipt. Remainder due 14 DAYS PRIOR TO EVENT. Producer reserves right

to withhold services if a signed Agreement Memo and payments are not received in accordance with this schedule. Terms on unpaid additional amounts: 2% per month after 7 days.

2. Commencement of this event and physical delivery of this contract constitute verification of an oral agreement and bind all parties to the terms contained herein.

3. Cancellation Policy: Greater than 60 days prior to event, no penalty; 59 - 30 days prior to event, 25% of contracted amount; 29 - 15 days prior to event, 50% of contracted amount; 14 days or less prior to event, 100% of contracted amount.

4. It is agreed that in case of emergency or act of God preventing act(s) or supplier(s) scheduled from appearing, suitable substitutions may be made, subject to Client approval.

5. This binding agreement between parties hereto shall be governed by all rules and regulations of unions involved and is subject to the return of signed contracts by act(s)/supplier(s). Client shall be notified within 14 days of the date of this contract of any act/supplier's non-acceptance.

6. It is understood that any props or equipment utilized for the above event shall be considered as rentals and any loss or damage caused by the Client's guests may be billed at replacement cost by the Producer. Costs of staging, electrical power hookup, facilities, and copyright license fees are not included in above prices unless otherwise specified.

7. This binding agreement between parties hereto shall be governed by the laws of the Province of British Columbia, Canada and any action initiated to enforce the terms of this contract by or against the Producer or by or against act(s)/supplier(s), will have its sole and exclusive forum in the City of Vancouver, British Columbia, Canada.

ACCEPTED BY CLIENT _____

ABC EVENT COMPANY LTD. _____

**ABC Event Company Ltd.**
**1234 Main St.**
**Vancouver, BC V4R 5T7 Canada**
**Fax: 123-456-7890**
**Phone: 123-567-8901**
**E-mail: info@abceventcompany.com**

Sample Form 19-2: Medium Complex Client Contract

## SERVICES AGREEMENT

This agreement for services is between ABC Event Company Ltd. and the Client indicated below. This agreement is effective on the date last signed below.

1. **Services**. ABC Event Company Ltd. will perform the services noted on Exhibit A attached ("Services") for the Event and on the date(s) and location indicated thereon. Client's responsibilities in connection with the Services are also outlined on Exhibit A. Client acknowledges that ABC Event Company Ltd. will commence providing the Services upon execution hereof by both parties.

2. **Compensation**. As compensation for the Services, Client will pay ABC Event Company Ltd. the compensation indicated on Exhibit A ("Compensation"). Compensation does [not] include the costs associated with all entertainment, sub-contracted services, equipment rentals, and the like to be provided and/or coordinated by ABC Event Company Ltd. Such costs, if not included in the Compensation, shall be paid directly by Client when due.

3. **Contact Persons**. The Contact Persons for the Services for ABC Event Company Ltd. and for the Client are listed on Exhibit A. ABC Event Company Ltd. may assign any one or more of its representatives to perform the Services.

4. **Proprietary Contacts.** Client understands that ABC Event Company Ltd. is in the business of event planning and coordination and as such, its contacts, suppliers, contractors, entertainers, and the like ("Proprietary Contacts") are considered by ABC Event Company Ltd. as proprietary and a valuable business asset. Client agrees that for a two (2) year period after the date hereof Client will not directly or indirectly contact, except through ABC Event Company Ltd., any of the Proprietary Contacts. If Client should breach this provision, as liquidated damages therefore, Client shall promptly pay ABC Event Company Ltd. its then current commission for the type of service provided to the Client by or through the Proprietary Contact.

5. **Limitation of Liability.** Client understands that all of the Proprietary Contacts are independent contractors to ABC Event Company Ltd. ABC Event Company Ltd. will make reasonable efforts to secure quality Proprietary Contacts for the Event but cannot guarantee the quality of performance and/or services of such contractors and will not be liable for such contractors' acts, errors and/or omissions including their fail-

ure to provide the required services. Further, if ABC Event Company Ltd. is providing any third party products as part of the Services, ABC EVENT COMPANY LTD. MAKES NO REPRESENTATIONS OR WARRANTIES OF ANY KIND, EXPRESS OR IMPLIED, INCLUDING BUT NOT LIMITED TO THE WARRANTIES OF MERCHANTABILITY AND FITNESS FOR A PARTICULAR PURPOSE, WITH REGARD TO THOSE PRODUCTS. In any event, ABC Event Company Ltd.'s liability for any and all claims shall be limited to the amount of Compensation actually earned by ABC Event Company Ltd. from the item giving rise to the claim and under no circumstances shall ABC Event Company Ltd. be liable for indirect or consequential damages, including lost profits.

6. **Bad Weather; Unforeseen Events.** ABC Event Company Ltd. shall not be responsible for events beyond its reasonable control which negatively affect the Event or the Services, including but not limited to: rain, snow, fire, flood, earthquake, lightning, or other acts of God; acts of civil or military authority; wars; riots; strikes; and sabotage. In all such cases, the Client shall remain responsible for the Compensation payable to ABC Event Company Ltd.

7. **Insurance.** Client will maintain general liability insurance for the Event in the amount of at least $1,000,000 per occurrence naming ABC Event Company Ltd. as an additional insured. If requested, Client will promptly deliver a Certificate of Insurance indicating the above to ABC Event Company Ltd.

8. **Termination.** Either party may terminate this Agreement at any time upon thirty days written notice to the other. In the event of such early termination, ABC Event Company Ltd. shall be entitled to the Compensation for the Services performed through the effective date of termination, including but not limited to compensation for time spent, contractors engaged, deposits made, and the like.

The parties have executed this Agreement as a document under seal to be construed in accordance with the laws of the State of Louisiana, USA.

x_____          x_____

Arthur Fancypants, President          Joan Getalife

ABC EVENT COMPANY LTD.                 CLIENT

**ABC Event Company Ltd.**

**1234 Main St.**

**New Orleans, LA USA 76543**
**Fax: 123-456-7890**
**Phone: 123-567-8901**
**E-mail: info@abceventcompany.com**

Sample Form 19-3: EXHIBIT A to SERVICES AGREEMENT

CLIENT:

EVENT:

DATE(S):

LOCATION:

DESCRIPTION OF SERVICES
PROVIDED BY ABC EVENT COMPANY LTD.:


DESCRIPTION OF CLIENT
RESPONSIBILITIES:


COMPENSATION AND TERMS
OF PAYMENT:


CONTACT PERSONS:


ABC EVENT COMPANY LTD: Arthur Fancypants: 123-456-7890

CLIENT: Joan Getalife: 123-765-4321

**ABC Event Company Ltd.**
**1234 Main St.**
**New Orleans, LA USA 76543**
**Fax: 123-456-7890**
**Phone: 123-567-8901**
**E-mail: info@abceventcompany.com**

Sample Form 19-4: Artist/Supplier Contract

## STANDARD FORM CONTRACT

The Undersigned engages the Artist(s)/Supplier(s) named hereinafter for the engagement/ work described below, subject to all of the provisions contained herein or attached to this contract, which conditions are hereby a part of the agreement:

**Name of Act/Supplier:** The Best Party Band     **Contact Person:** James Smith
**Address:** 12345 - 57A Avenue                                   **Phone:** 345-987-5432
            New York, NY 59345                                    **Fax:** 345-987-3210

**Performance Date:** December 7, 2002     **Show Time:** 9:00 PM

**Production No:** 02120701                                **Client/Sponsor:** Honest Jake's
            Insurance Co.

**Type of Event:** Christmas Party

**Performance Location:** Rest Easy Hotel     **Room:** Ballroom
            49th Street
            New Harbor, NY 56784

**Report to:**   Barry Jones <u>**1/2 HOUR BEFORE SHOWTIME/START OF EVENT**</u>

**Fee:**   $3,800.00  +  Tax: $266.00  =  $4,066.00

**Details of Performance/Work:**

The Best Party Band: 7-piece band to play for dancing, 9:00pm - 1:00am.  Fee includes all sound and lights. Setup and sound check time TBA. A green room has been requested.

1.   It is understood that the artist(s)/supplier(s) execute(s) this contract as an independent contractor(s) and is/are not an employee(s) of ABC Event Company Ltd. As such, artist(s)/supplier(s) understand(s) that it is his/her/their responsibility to submit all CPP,

WCB, and income tax payments as required by the Governments of British Columbia and Canada.

2.  Artist(s)/supplier(s) must contact ABC Event Company Ltd. prior to engagement/commencing work for any change of instructions.

3.  Any overtime must be authorized by Client, and any problems or disputes must be reported to ABC Event Company Ltd. within 24 hours following engagement/completion of work.

4.  Artist(s)/supplier(s) is/are responsible for own equipment, appropriate costumes/attire, and control of performance/work, as well as all matters of public safety. This includes holding liability and equipment insurance.

5.  Artist(s)/supplier(s) shall not consume food or drink in performing area unless authorized by client.

6.  All contracts are subject to receipt of signed Agreement Memo by Producer from Client. In case of emergency or act of God preventing artist(s)/supplier(s) from appearing/commencing work, suitable substitution may be made.

7.  ABC Event Company Ltd. cancellation policy is: greater than 60 days prior to event, no payment; 59 - 30 days prior to event, 25% of contracted amount; 29 - 15 days prior to event, 50% of contracted amount; 14 days or less prior to event, 100% of contracted amount. However, if Client fails to pay and a settlement cannot be reached, ABC Event Company Ltd. will endeavor to negotiate a fair settlement with artist/supplier when possible.

8.  It is understood that all future engagements/work resulting from above performance/work (e.g. request made directly to artist/supplier by Client or by one of Client's guests) up to 18 months following the date of this engagement/work, shall be contracted by ABC Event Company Ltd.

In Witness whereof, we have signed this Agreement on the day and year written below.

Date:_____Date:_____

Act/Supplier:                          ABC Event Company Ltd.

By:_____By:_____

PLEASE SIGN AND RETURN ONE COPY WITHIN 14 DAYS TO:

**ABC Event Company Ltd.**
**1234 Main St.**
**Vancouver, BC V4R 5T7 Canada**
**Fax: 123-456-7890**
**Phone: 123-567-8901**
**E-mail: info@abceventcompany.com**

Sample Form 19-5: Addendum to All Contracts with Sub-Contractors, Suppliers, and Artists Working for ABC Event Company Ltd.

In order to present the most professional image possible and to maintain good working relationships with our clients and venue staffs, we ask for your co-operation in adhering to the following guidelines:

1. Once you have signed a contract with ABC Event Company Ltd. you are considered to be working for ABC Event Company Ltd., and no other company, whether it is your own or someone else's. In such capacity, you will be expected to conduct yourself professionally and with courtesy at all times. When first contacting clients or venue staff, please identify yourself by name and the fact that you are representing ABC Event Company Ltd. If, for any reason, disputes arise over any matter, ABC Event Company Ltd. must be notified as soon as possible if no company representative is on site.

2. Prior to any load-in of equipment or decor and prior to any setup of equipment or décor at a venue, the crew supervisor will report to the Banquet Captain in charge or to the appropriate venue manager to ascertain:
   - the correct location to park vehicles for unloading and how long the vehicle may remain there
   - the correct route to take to load in equipment
   - any scheduling problems
   - any special requirements (e.g. request for no noise, etc.).

   The same procedure as in (2) shall be followed for equipment strike at the end of an event.

3. The minimum dress for all technical personnel (e.g. decorators, technicians, and laborers) shall be clean T-shirt and work pants (same for males or females). Whenever possible, all personnel shall wear a clean ABC Event Company Ltd. T-shirt (available at no charge at the company office). Technicians (e.g. audio and lighting) on duty at events shall wear shirts, ties, sports jacket, and slacks as a minimum. Performers shall always wear appropriate stage attire (except when a costume is called for). Blue jeans and scruffy clothes are not acceptable.

4. All technical staff, decorators, and performers shall re-check the details of their contracts with ABC Event Company Ltd. at least 48 hours prior to an event.

5. For those required to meet a schedule (e.g. setup of decor), a re-check of contract details is vital, and any deadlines that are not met may result in financial penalty. Please keep in mind that hotel and venue staffs invariably require at least one or two hours with a clear room to prepare for an event after all decor and equipment has been set up.

6. Be mindful of requests by hotel and venue staff. For example, a request for no nails in the walls means just that! A discovery later on that a simple request has been ignored can only be detrimental to both ABC Event Company Ltd. and you as a subcontractor.

7. You are responsible for all cleanup of mess resulting from your particular responsibility area (e.g. decorators should vacuum or sweep all areas after setup and after strike, technicians should ensure all tape, wires and other miscellaneous small pieces are not left behind, and performers should ensure their stage or performance area is left clean).

8. BE PREPARED! Ensure - before you leave home - that you not only have all necessary equipment but also enough of all items. Use a checklist. Do not expect the hotel or venue to supply extension cords, duct tape, tools, ladders, vacuum cleaners, brooms, lights for music stands, or other essential items that are your responsibility. Asking to borrow equipment makes both you and ABC Event Company Ltd. look disorganized.

9. Consumption of Clients' alcohol or food when on duty at an event is not permitted. Do not help yourself to either unless specifically invited to do so by the client or by ABC Event Company Ltd. staff. Any subcontractor, supplier, or performer found or reported to be under the influence of alcohol or drugs at an event shall no longer be hired by ABC Event Company Ltd.

**This addendum shall be considered part of your contract with ABC Event Company Ltd.**

Date:_____Date:_____

Act/Supplier:                                      ABC Event Company Ltd.

By:_____By:_____

**ABC Event Company Ltd.**
**1234 Main St.**
**Vancouver, BC V4R 5T7 Canada**
**Fax: 123-456-7890**
**Phone: 123-567-8901**
**E-mail: info@abceventcompany.com**

Sample Form 19-6: Alternate Artist Contract

## ARTIST CONFIRMATION CONTRACT

Artist Name:

Artist Address:

Work Phone:                                          Fax:

Home Phone:

IN ACCORDANCE WITH OUR CONVERSATION, YOU ARE TO PROVIDE US WITH THE FOLLOWING:

Artist/Group:

Date of Engagement:

Performance Location

Report Time:

Show Time:

Event Type:

Clothing:

Fee:

Facility Contact Name and Phone Number:

Remarks and/or Details of Performance or Work:

As a performer, I agree to refer any and all offers for future bookings resulting from the above engagement to the producer who placed me in this assignment. In the event of overtime, I will report it to ABC Event Company Ltd. immediately following the engagement for billing and payment purposes. Any additional time will be prorated and billed to the client by ABC Event Company Ltd.

PLEASE NOTE: In signing this form, I agree that I am being engaged as an independent contractor. I am aware that ABC Event Company Ltd. issues 1099's for this purpose. I have read and agreed to the additional terms and conditions on the next page.

(Please initial)_____

Make Check Payable to:_____

Social Security No: _____Federal ID No:_____

Are you incorporated?     YES:_____NO:_____

_____     _____
Artist Signature                      ABC Event Company Ltd., Signature

Please sign the contract and return it to ABC Event Company Ltd. Please see Additional Terms and Conditions on the reverse of this contract. Retain a copy for your records.

**ABC Event Company Ltd.**
**1234 Main St.**
**New Orleans, LA USA 76543**
**Fax: 123-456-7890**
**Phone: 123-567-8901**
**E-mail: info@abceventcompany.com**

Sample Form 19-7: Alternate Addendum to All Artist Contracts

## ADDITIONAL TERMS AND CONDITIONS

1. Do not discuss fees with Client.

2. Payment will be made through the ABC Event Company Ltd. office on the first and fifteenth of each month. If you play on the first, you will be paid on-the fifteenth of the mouth. If you play on the fifteenth, you will be paid on the first of the next month. Do not try to negotiate overtime rates with the Client. It is your responsibility to report any overtime played to your respective producer immediately following the engagement.

3. Unless invited, we ask that you do not drink on the job. Many clients complain that the musicians take advantage of the buffet lines and open bars - at their expense.

4. Be on time: Give yourself plenty of time in order to start the engagement promptly!

5. Look your best. Costumes or tuxedo attire are requested unless otherwise stated in this agreement.

6. Only ABC Event Company Ltd. cards are to be handed out at ABC Event Company Ltd. events. To do otherwise will seriously jeopardize your credibility and future work potential through this office.

7. This contract is not subject to cancellation without written agreement of both parties and notification delivered in writing to ABC Event Company Ltd.

8. Performer(s) agree to refer any and all offers of future engagements resulting from the above engagement to ABC Event Company Ltd.

9. It is expressly agreed that ABC Event Company Ltd. acts herein as Producer, and is not responsible for any act of commission or omission on the client part of either Client or Performer.

10. Be sure to insert your social security number or federal employment ID numbers. Failure to do so may cause a delay in payment for a completed engagement.

11. This contract cannot be assigned or transferred without the prior written consent of the Producer.

**ABC Event Company Ltd.**
**1234 Main St.**
**New Orleans, LA USA 76543**
**Fax: 123-456-7890**
**Phone: 123-567-8901**
**E-mail: info@abceventcompany.com**

# 20

## Production Management

### PART ONE: IN THE EVENT COORDINATION PHASE

What exactly is production management? Production management is the task of bringing all the technical - and many non-technical - event elements together. This can include, audio, A-V, lighting, décor, entertainment, staging, stage management, scheduling, rehearsals, and scripting. Much of this does not truly occur until the actual event or immediately prior to the event during setup; however, there are some elements that must be prepared long before the event itself and which the event planner must consider even before contracting. The most important such elements include:

### Venue Details

Whether it is an outdoor or indoor site, the people in charge of the site must be kept informed of the plans for event setup and strike. This can only occur during the event coordination phase. The following details are part of this planning:

- What type of power is available and where is it located, what is the cost for tie-in and how will it be tied in? Usually - but not always - lighting and audio prefer power tie-in near or behind the main stage.
- Is adequate staging available and can it be set up in a timely manner? Is there a cost for staging as well and is the surface appropriate for the show? Is it steady? Is a wheelchair ramp necessary and if so, is one available from the venue or must one be constructed or brought in?
- What time is room or site access?
- Are there any specific restrictions about installation of equipment or décor such as no nails in walls?

- What will the venue be doing during event setup? There can be no clashes between tech personnel and venue staff, such as setting up tables at the same time as lighting is being flown.
- Is there easy freight elevator and loading dock access and how long does it take to move from the loading dock to the event location? Will all equipment and props fit into the freight elevator or will they have to be brought in via an alternate route and perhaps even at an alternate time?
- Are there green rooms readily available with all necessary amenities for tech personnel and performers?
- What time is strike and will there be any clashes when loading out?

## Site/Venue Layout and CADD (Computer — Aided Design and Drafting)

Unless the event is very simple and has no décor or minimal staging, draw a floor or site plan to scale. Even if it is hand-drawn, it is at least a simple guide. It's too easy to make mistakes without it. There are many excellent CADD programs on the market today and they are easy to use. Some even have the capability of full, three-dimensional (3-D) rendering, QuickTime movie fly-through videos, and lighting renderings for the entire venue and for staging. Two well-known programs include Vectorworks (rapidly becoming an industry standard) and AutoCAD. As well, many less complex - but quite usable - programs are included with some of the event planning software available on the market. The benefit to using this type of program is that it can be easily and quickly changed to match any changes in event plans. For example, table templates can be loaded quickly in order to illustrate the effect of adding or deleting tables, all with correctly pre-determined spacing.

With the pace and complexity of today's events, and often very tight physical tolerances, hand drawing just no longer cuts the mustard. Plate 1 is a very simple example (drawn in Vectorworks) of a small dinner in a hotel ballroom. Plate 2 illustrates what can be done in three dimensions when the full capability of CADD is used to render a scene. This example also uses a specific rendering add-on to the basic CADD program that enables different lighting effects to be accurately portrayed, incorporating very exact reflectivity and texture of surfaces and intensity of different light sources.

Note that a venue layout should be created as soon as possible once the basic details of the event are known. It can then be used as a planning tool for all participants including the venue itself, so that there is no room for error in setting up all the elements.

## Supplier Liaison

Much of the technical side of events involves considerable amounts of very specific equipment, particularly in the areas of audio, lighting, and A-V. Prior to the event, the entire list of contracted equipment should be reviewed for adequacy to ensure it is appropriate for the specific job. For example, it is very easy to bring in the wrong focal length light fixtures and not be able to focus correctly on a wall or surface because the lighting company did not have a good understanding of what was needed. Better to get this straightened out **before** the event rather than **at** the event.

The setup schedule for all suppliers should be thoroughly reviewed in detail to ensure they will be at the event in sufficient time to accomplish their setup with the assigned personnel and also to ensure there will be no conflicts with other suppliers or venue staff.

As a final part of supplier liaison, the planner should check that the best-qualified personnel will actually be at the event operating their respective equipment. A simple example here is on the audio side. Often, A-V companies provide highly qualified technicians who are very well qualified for operating equipment for speakers, such as lectern microphones, wireless lavalier microphones, projectors, and such, but have never mixed audio for a dance band or sophisticated stage show before. This can result in disaster if that technician is on the job when the show aspect is the most important element of the event. It would be better to hire an audio company that has extensive entertainment experience than try to "wing it" with the A-V company.

## Planning the Show

This is the part where you get to create the excitement! If the planner does not do this, then either a good production manager or choreographer must actually put the show together. This involves several elements:

- Creating the excitement. This is the actual design of the entertainment and stage portion of the event, whether or not it includes speeches, awards, special effects, entertainment, and/or other elements. You need to answer the following questions:

  o What is your concept for the show itself?
  o How will it flow and how will changes be made and incorporated overall into it?
  o Are there different parts of the show that must be made to fit without being too obvious?
  o How will it come together?

o   How long will it take and must anything be added or deleted from it to improve it or make it fit within the time allowed? Remember that for most corporate or any other entertainment shows other than a pure concert, 50 to 60 minutes is as long as any show should last.

o   Does it fit with the client's vision?

o   Once you have developed the show, you must commit it to paper in the form of a running order and then decide if more scripting is required and what sort of rehearsals are required to make sure it happens as you and your client have planned.

- Scripting. Many events, especially corporate events that involve awards, speeches, complex A-V presentations, and elaborate entertainment shows, frequently require scripts for MCs or even for the entertainment show itself. Although the event planner does not necessarily need to be able to write the script, it is one of the elements that must be considered in the coordination phase as the length and content may impact how the show is structured. Often nowadays, the entire script is incorporated into the A-V portion of the show and might very well be all pre-recorded.

- Rehearsals. Like scripting, most events if even remotely complex, require a rehearsal of some sort. Many speakers and VIPs usually want to take time to rehearse and try out the A-V systems, to set up personal or portable computers for PowerPoint presentations, to check lighting levels, and to determine timing. In addition, entertainment shows may need anything from a full dress rehearsal to at minimum a talk-through with the Technical Director and stage managers to ensure everyone is in the right place at the right time and knows what the proper cues are. All these requirements must be considered in the coordination phase so that setup and event schedules take them into account and that nothing is left to chance.

- Scheduling. After liaising with all suppliers and venue staff, the final segment in the coordination phase is to create and issue a detailed event schedule that includes setup and strike details, plus a more specific show running order for the event itself. This outlines in intimate detail, all the specific cues for actions during the event, from the president coming to the stage to give a speech, to video and audio cues, to the exact entrances and exits of performers. This document becomes the Bible for the event planner and the Production Manager or Technical Director as the event unfolds. It is to this document that the show is run. This will be examined in the next phase, Event Execution.

Note also that for more complex, large public or large private events, project management software is sometimes useful as it allows for conflicts in scheduling and offers options to get around them. Microsoft Project is an example of such a sophisticated program. See Table 20-3 for a sample of a typical small event schedule and running order.

# PART TWO: IN THE EVENT EXECUTION PHASE

Setup for, and running of, the actual event involves a great deal of technical work in all the areas of staging, audio, lighting, A-V, special effects, and often others. For a typical indoor event with an entertainment and staging component, some of the more important considerations throughout this time are the following:

## Staging

Making a stage useful requires an understanding of some basic concepts:

- Terminology. Special events use the same terminology as the theater. Quite simply, this means that everything is considered from the point of view of a person (e.g. performer/actor) who is on the stage. Thus, as you look at the stage from the audience, everything is reversed. The front of the stage is considered downstage, the back of the stage is considered upstage (in the theater, sometimes stages are "raked" or slanted up towards the back to give the illusion of depth), the left side of the stage is stage right, and the right of the stage is stage left.

- Functionality. Stages only become functional with planning, taking into consideration:

  o Size. Know beforehand the maximum number of people that will be on the stage at any given time and plan the size accordingly. Ensure there is enough space for tables or chairs if there will be a panel discussion, group photograph, or tables for holding prizes and awards. If there will be entertainment, ensure all performers are aware of the stage size and what the exact amount of available space will be at the time of their performance. They have to know if a podium or table or other element will be obstructing their performance.

o Traffic flow. Anticipate everything that will happen on the stage from the start of the show to the end. Go through the event completely in your mind's eye and know what is going to happen before it does. Will there be obstructions? Is the podium going to be in the way of sight lines? Would it be better to have two podiums for greater efficiency? Will the lectern(s) or other fixtures on the stage have to be moved or replaced at any time throughout the event, how will this be done and how long will it take? Are there any microphone cords or other possible obstructions on the stage? Which side will people enter from and which side will they exit? Will they enter or exit from the rear of the stage (upstage) or through a stage set or wings? Are the stairs in the right place for easy access? Are they safe and with railings or marked with obvious yellow tape at the edges? Is there easy access through the audience to the stage or will it be more efficient to bring presenters or winners up to the side of the stage well before they are due to be on? Is there easy access to the stage for performers so that they cannot be seen before they perform? Is there a backstage area or wings where people can prepare for their time onstage? Is the stage wheelchair-accessible if anyone who is disabled will be participating?

o Sight lines. There really should be no reason for everyone in an audience not to see the stage. If guests cannot see, then the event has a design flaw. Either there are too many people for the size of the venue, the stage is too small or too low, or there are obstructive décor and structural elements present that should have been considered in the initial planning of the event. Nevertheless, even with experienced event planners and production managers, problems do occur, usually due to limited budgets. Problems can generally be overcome by:

- keeping table centers low enough and narrow enough to allow a good view of the stage (really only important if there are many things planned for the stage);
- raising the height of the stage if there is a large and spread-out audience;
- keeping tables and chairs in front of the front (downstage) edge of the stage;
- "flying" audio and lighting to avoid obstructions from speaker cabinets and lighting trees;
- avoiding placing chairs or dining tables behind venue structural columns or architectural elements.

## Stage Sets and Backdrops

Stages can be enhanced by the proper design of sets that make them a strong focal point in an event. To do this requires preliminary thinking about:

- Design. Elaborateness of design usually depends on the purpose of the event. If it is a simple theme night, and there will be just entertainment on the stage, the design might be very decorative and incorporate total theming, such as a soft backdrop of a western town or a hard wall of a false-fronted western street. If the stage is more for an opening ceremony, awards show or a conference technical plenary session, then it might be much more functional and incorporate a conference themed message along with audio-visual elements of screen(s) and/or video walls.

- The message. Because the stage set or backdrop is often the most obvious visual element in an event and the one area where the audience's attention is focused for most of the time, it should be put to optimum use in conveying a message or a theme. For example, a stage set and/or the screens or video walls can be used to acknowledge event sponsors, to project live video (IMAG or image magnification), to emphasize a meeting theme, to project important messages such as schedules, or even to hide other event sessions.

- Other considerations. In general, it is always a good idea to provide stage wings either on the stage or on the floor beside the stage, to allow for unseen preparation of entertainment performances and/or awards presentations. It looks more professional and permits privacy. If budget is a concern, black velour drape hung using continuously extendable uprights is a classy alternative to a more expensive hard wall as a stage backdrop and for wings. Also, bare stages can be dressed very effectively using large potted florals around lecterns, along the front of the stage, on the corners and in front of the backdrop. Finally, for a cheap and effective method of projecting a company name or theme on a backdrop, consider the use of specially cut "gobo" projections from a lighting company.

## Staffing

Most shows incorporating lighting, audio, A-V, and often entertainment, also have a requirement to provide technical staff from all these areas to run the show, especially if there are many awards, presentations, speeches, and/or entertainment segments. While Production Managers should be generally familiar with how each specialty functions and what the equipment does, a detailed knowledge is not necessary, especially now that technology is changing so fast. However, if the Production Manager will be calling the show, he should have voice communication with all the players, including followspot operators, audio engineer, lighting engineer, A-V engineer (especially if complex equipment such as multiple PowerPoint presentations, video wall, teleconferencing, and video tape changes will be involved), and stage managers.

All technical personnel should be fully conversant with the entire show and be familiar with the total running order. All should be prepared ahead of time to make the appropriate changes when the time comes in the show. Examples include microphone changes and re-sets onstage, special lighting cues for performers, CD/mini-disc/tape changes, video wall cues, switching equipment (e.g. video wall to PowerPoint to straight video) cues, performer cues, and followspot cues.

All personnel should be extremely familiar with the equipment under their control. This means that they should be able to analyze and fix any problems very quickly. Not only that, but with today's complex equipment, they should be able to program it for maximum effect. A good example is intelligent lighting such as Technobeams or Vari-Lites that can be programmed to follow moving people ahead of time if the path will not vary much (e.g. walking up to a stage). This can be an easy way to eliminate a followspot and operator.

It is always wise to schedule a complete rehearsal or at minimum a full talk-through of the event with all technical personnel before the event begins. In this way, everyone knows exactly what to expect and has an opportunity to bring up any potential problem areas. Shows also run much more smoothly when everyone literally is on the same page and this means they should all have a copy of a complete script or at a minimum, a complete and detailed running order. It is the Production Manager's responsibility to produce these documents.

Besides technical staff, stage managers form an essential component of a complex show. They can save much time, effort and stress, and are primarily used to:

- alert speakers ahead of time and prepare them by bringing them to the stage holding area;
- physically assist with stage changeovers;
- take performers to and from Green Rooms;
- cue performers, speakers and others who will be using the stage;
- keep the show flowing.

They should always be in voice contact with the Production Manager either by intercom or radio.

## Communications

Production Managers usually communicate using either two-way radios with multiple channels (if walls or distance preclude using intercom) or intercom, most notably equipment made by Clear-Com, also with multiple channels. Radios generally come with the option of a headset and microphone to allow privacy. Clear-Com units come with headset microphones and can be either wired to a fixed station, or completely wireless with a belt pack and antenna. The current industry standard seems to be Clear-Com. The equipment has a press-to-talk function or a continuous talk, hands-free function.

In addition, there is other equipment that has only a one-way talk function called IFB ("in-ear fold-back" or "in-ear monitor"). This is used by broadcasters and increasingly by informed Production Managers and Technical Directors to communicate with people onstage such as MCs, hosts, and musicians. It consists of a small earpiece with a wire and a receiver pack that must be affixed to the person on a belt or dress on their back out of sight of the audience. It is an extremely useful item if sudden changes must be made (e.g. shorten or lengthen a presentation, change something due to a mistaken technical cue, etc), and the Production Manager does not want to make the mistake or change obvious to the audience.

## Radio Protocol

General guidelines for using a radio or intercom are simple. There is no magic to it. Press to talk, say what you have to in a minimum number of words, then take your finger off the button and ensure the green light is out! To get someone's attention, make it simple and obvious (e.g. "Dave calling Susan," or "Susan from Dave"). To acknowledge someone calling you, again stick with simplicity (e.g. "Go for Susan"). To acknowledge an instruction use simple code (e.g. "10-4") or just say "understood."

Other things to keep in mind: keep idle chatter to a minimum; don't cough into a live mic; keep volume loud enough to hear but not too loud for others; and let others know when you are going "off comm." There are some codes that occasionally may prove useful in noisy, crowded, or public events:

- Radio code numbers. Although for the majority of events most Production Managers work on, security radio codes as used by police will not be necessary, sometimes it is useful to have them and it is definitely a bonus if the event is a large public one. They are:

Table 20-1: Radio Code Numbers

| One | Major incident |
| Two | Reportable incident |
| Three | Coordination meeting |
| Four | Lost Child |
| Five | VIP/Cash Escort |
| 10 – 4 | Acknowledgement |
| 10 – 7 | Out of service (i.e. off comm.) |
| 10 – 8 | Back in service (i.e. back on comm.) |
| 10 – 9 | Say again |
| 10 – 20 | State your location |
| 10 – 21 | Call *** by telephone |
| 10 – 26 | Detaining suspect |
| 10 – 30 | Improper use of radio |
| 10 – 50 | Transmission is good |
| 10 – 52 | Ambulance needed |
| 10 – 100 | Bomb/major threat |

*Note: Never say, "lost child" or "cash" over the radio during a public event!*

- Radio code alphabet. As with the number codes, usually most of us will not need them. However, they can be very useful if transmission is difficult or there is any misunderstanding amongst alphabet letters (e.g. b, c, d, g, p, etc).

Table 20-2: Radio Code Alphabet

| A ........... | ALPHA | N ........... | NOVEMBER |
| B ........... | BRAVO | O ........... | OSCAR |
| C ........... | CHARLIE | P ........... | PAPA |
| D ........... | DELTA | Q ........... | QUEBEC |
| E ........... | ECHO | R ........... | ROMEO |
| F ........... | FOXTROT | S ........... | SIERRA |
| G ........... | GOLF | T ........... | TANGO |
| H ........... | HOTEL | U ........... | UNIFORM |
| I ........... | INDIA | V ........... | VICTOR |
| J ........... | JULIET | W ........... | WHISKEY |
| K ........... | KILO | X ........... | X-RAY |
| L ........... | LIMA | Y ........... | YANKEE |
| M ........... | MIKE | Z ........... | ZULU |

## Calling a Show

For a show to run smoothly, the Technical Director, Production Manager, or "Show Caller" needs to be comfortable with all aspects of the equipment, personnel, and event. Some considerations are:

- Communication channel assignment. Everyone has a personal preference. On Clear-Com there are multiple channels and a Production Manager (PM) needs to decide which technical personnel must talk to each other throughout the show. My personal choice is to have one main channel that incorporates the most important parts of the show (e.g. PM, stage managers, and audio or PM, stage managers, and video wall, etc). Depending on the show, sometimes lighting for example has a couple of follow-spots and lots of separate cues. They might be better off on their own channel so as not to interrupt the other calls, especially if they are intimately familiar with the show and really need no formal cues for each major stage change. Likewise, sometimes an orchestra leader may not want to be disturbed except for specific cues relating to him, in which case he needs a separate channel as well.

- The show. The secret is to get a flow established. Try to warn each person ahead of time when it is their turn to do something. In the example below, the Production Manager or Technical Director (TD) is "Doug," who is "calling the show", the Stage Manager (SM) is "John," and the Video Director is VD.

  o  TD: "Doug for John."
  o  SM: "Go for John."
  o  TD: "Standby with Mr. Smith at stage right and put him onstage right after this speaker finishes."
  o  SM: "10 – 4."
  o  TD: "John from Doug - Mr. Smith onstage Go."
  o  SM: "Mr. Smith is onstage."
  o  TD: "Lights – Change to a blue wash for Mr. Smith Go."
  o  TD: "Video – are you ready with the next clip after Mr. Smith – it's the clip for the new sales program?"
  o  VD: "Standing by with video clip of new program."
  o  TD: "Video clip of new program Go."
  o  And so on as per the show running order.

Note that overall there is a standard sequence for giving verbal cues:

o   "Stand-by Sound Cue 19" (Stand-by first).
o   "Sound Cue 19 Go" (Go last).

Repeat this same order for the next series of presenters or stage segment and try to keep it going throughout the event. The key is to anticipate and know exactly what must be done at least four or five steps ahead of where you are in the show running order or script. Give everyone lots of time to get to their assigned positions and complete their tasks. Check off each item on the running order or script as it finishes. Try to keep calm and not get flustered if things go wrong. Think logically. Keep in mind that, like an airplane taking off and landing, the first and last 10 minutes of the show are the most critical and they are the times when something is most likely to go wrong. If you are new to the game, start on a really simple show and work your way up from there.

- Location. Again, everyone has a preference. I prefer to call a complex show from the rear of the room from a central communication station that is connected to all the technical people involved, and from where I can see the whole picture. Other times, if the show involves a lot of entertainment that might be entering and leaving from different parts of the venue, I work better calling the show from a wireless station that gives me the flexibility to move around and change the way the show flows if I see it needs it, or to talk directly to an entertainer or presenter.

## KEY POINTS OF PRODUCTION MANAGEMENT

Anticipation is without question the key to good production management. Try to visualize everything that will be happening during your event. Walk through the entire event from start to finish in your head, including where and when guests and performers will be moving. If anything looks like it might be wrong or even has the potential to go wrong, address it before the event, because it probably will go wrong if you don't.

Ensure that power and staging are adequate and in place well before the rest of the technical setup. The last thing you want is for technicians and decorators tripping over venue staff trying to put a stage in place or waiting for power that should have been installed hours ago.

Besides that, venues will often charge more for such items as power if it is requested onsite.

Allow ample time for setup. This is frequently where inexperience causes disasters. There are just too many small things that can get off-track if people must work within a serious time crunch. It is far better to be too early and wait around than to still be doing a sound check as guests enter the event space.

Keep updated and firm schedules of setup, event running order, and strike. Stick to the schedules and ensure that all people involved with the event are on the distribution list. This includes venue staff, performers, all technical people, and of course, your client.

Know all requirements and technical riders for performers. This can include everything from stage plots and sound and lighting requirements, to dressing room riders. Be aware of the excessive riders of some celebrity talent and try to negotiate out all except what is reasonable.

Ensure that there are dressing rooms of adequate size and privacy for performers. Don't forget that some shows require quick-change areas close to the main stage such as dance shows where fast costume changes are part of the show. Be prepared to pay extra to set these up properly.

Ensure you have adequate and capable stage management in place to run the show. In addition, ensure that adequate communication equipment is available for the stage managers. The best kind is wireless headset equipment like Clear-Com which enables you to talk and listen without anyone else hearing the conversation and to move about the venue freely and still be in communication.

Rehearse your show whenever possible. Even the smallest show can benefit from some kind of quick run-through. If the show and event are complex, plan for at least a pre-event talk-through with the key participants, including venue staff, performers, sound and lighting techs, and client.

Have contingencies in place for any unavoidable changes. Know how to react and what you will do before they happen. This goes along with anticipation but is the last and unfortunately very important step. For example, know how to compensate for a performer who is late or does not show up. Having a plan just may save you from disaster. Try to see through the rough spots and keep smiling.

Use an individual or company that is conversant with the production of complex events if you feel you are in over your head. This will save much stress!

Table 20-3: Sample Combined Event Schedule and Show Running Order

**Preliminary Schedule for Gala Night**

| Time | Location | Description |
|------|----------|-------------|
| 8:00am - 6:00pm (April 23) | Enterprise Hall | Lighting and audio installation. Beginning installation of décor (linens on tables and chairs, ribbons on balcony). Plaza to have power available from 8:00am |
| 1:00 - 6:00pm | Enterprise Hall | Rigging for aerial circus acts (Plaza staff) |
| 6:00 - 8:00pm | Enterprise Hall | Stage installation |
| 8:00 - 10:00pm | Enterprise Hall | Lighting focus (at night) |
| 9:00am – Noon (April 24) | Enterprise Hall | Rehearsal for circus acts, sound checks, remainder of décor installation (table centers) |
| 4:00 - 5:00pm | Enterprise Hall | Sound check for Cameron Hood Quartet and Alex Elixir |
| 5:00 - 6:30pm | Enterprise Hall | Crew dinner break |
| 6:30 - 7:00pm | Enterprise Hall | Talk-through of show (audio, lights, SM's, client) |
| 6:30pm | Hotel Vancouver | Staging of Coaches, 6 @ 47 passengers |
| 7:00pm | Enterprise Hall | Sixuvus, Public Dreams Society, Elenna Hope, Alex Elixir, Todo, Cameron Hood Quartet, Rod Boss, Cirque Fantastic acts - report to Doug Matthews in Enterprise Hall |
| 7:00 PM | Hotel Vancouver | Loading of Coaches, 3 at a time and departure for Plaza of Nations. |
| 7:30pm | Parking Lot | Sixuvus standby |
| | Entrance Area | 2 Stiltwalkers and 2 costumed characters standby to lead guests to Reception in 2 processions |
| | Mezzanine | Elenna Hope, Todo, Cameron Hood Quartet, Rod Boss standby to greet guests |
| | Pre-Show Area | Alex Elixir and Capri standby to greet guests as they arrive |
| 7:45 - 8:00pm | Pre-Show Area and Parking Lot | Sixuvus, Public Dreams greet guests |
| 8:00 - 8:45pm | Enterprise Hall - Mezzanine | All performers mingling. Alex and Capri plus 2 stiltwalkers and 2 costumed characters join in. |

| | | |
|---|---|---|
| 8:30pm | Enterprise Hall - Mezzanine | Sixuvus plus all performers standby to lead guests to dinner |
| | | Cameron Hood Quartet break and re-set on main floor |
| | Main Floor | Triple Rope act standby on main floor |
| 8:45pm | Enterprise Hall - Mezzanine | Sixuvus, Alex and Capri, Public Dreams costumed characters, Rod Boss, Todo, all lead guests to dinner |
| 9:00pm | Enterprise Hall - Main Floor | Solo Triple Rope act after guests seated |
| 9:08pm | Enterprise Hall - Main Floor | Catering - pre-set first course |
| | | Cameron Hood Quartet play background music |
| | | Contortionist act standby |
| 9:30pm | Enterprise Hall - Main Floor | Contortionist act onstage after first course cleared |
| 9:40pm | Enterprise Hall - Main Floor | Catering serves second course |
| | | Cameron Hood Quartet play background music |
| | | Duo Aerial Curtain act standby |
| 10:10pm | Enterprise Hall - Main Floor | Duo Aerial Curtain act performs after second course cleared |
| 10:20pm | Enterprise Hall - Main Floor | Catering serves third course. Course is not cleared. |
| | | Cameron Hood Quartet play background music |
| | | Alex Elixir standby |
| | | Public Dreams torchbearers standby outside Enterprise Hall guest exit |
| 10:30pm | Parking Lot | Staging of Coaches in the Parking Lot |
| | Enterprise Hall - Main Floor | Alex Elixir performs onstage, then leads guests around room as Public Dreams torchbearers enter with torches and join in, then lead all guests to buses. |
| 10:40 - 11:00pm | Parking Lot | Loading of buses |
| 11:00pm - 2:00am | Enterprise Hall | Strike of all rigging, staging, décor, sound, lighting |

Table 20-4: Glossary of Production Terminology

| Item | Description |
|---|---|
| **AFM** | American Federation of Musicians. Union representing musicians in the USA and Canada. |
| **Back Curtain** | The two-piece, bi-parting, rear curtain; part of the cyc set. Also known as a rear curtain or backdrop. |
| **Backstage** | All areas related to, but not on, the stage, including dressing rooms, technical areas, etc. |
| **Blocking** | The process of arranging moves to be made by performers during a show, recorded by stage management in the prompt script. |
| **Boards** | Slang term for the stage floor. |
| **Breakaway** | Prop or item of furniture designed to break/shatter with impact. Breakaway furniture and some props are usually capable of restoration to be "broken" again. |
| **CADD** | Computer aided design and drafting. For special events, it is most often seen in two dimensions (2-D) and shows a plan or top view. It can also be shown in front (elevation) and side views in 2-D and in three dimensions (3-D) from a number of different perspectives. |
| **Call or Call Time** | 1. A notification of a working session (e.g. a rehearsal call or show call). <br> 2. The period of time to which the above call refers. (e.g. "Your call for tomorrow night's show is 6.55pm.") <br> 3. A request for a performer to come to the stage because an entrance is imminent. These are courtesy calls and should not be relied on by actors. (e.g. "This is your call for the finale Mr. Smith and Miss Jones.") <br> 4. An acknowledgement of applause (i.e. Curtain Call). <br> 5. The Technical Director (TD) or Deputy Stage Manager (DSM) on the book is said to be "calling the cues" or "calling the show." |
| **Cast** | All performers/participants in a show. |

| | |
|---|---|
| **Center Stage** | The middle portion of the stage, it has good sightlines to all seats of the auditorium or audience. |
| **Clearance** | Message passed to Stage Management from the Front of House Manager (or client in the case of special events) that the house is ready for the performance to begin. |
| **Commando Cloth** | Napped, inexpensive fabric, popular as studio backdrop and stage cyc set fabric; typically black. |
| **Cross-Over** | Corridor formed between a back curtain or backdrop and the rear wall, so performers or stagehands may cross from one side to the other of the stage unseen by the audience, usually while a show is in progress. |
| **Cue (Q)** | A point in a live show when a signal is given for some action to take place. |
| **Cue To Cue** | Cutting out action and dialogue between cues during a technical rehearsal, to save time. |
| **Cueing** | There is a standard sequence for giving verbal cues: |

- "Stand-by Sound Cue 19" (Stand-by first).
- "Sound Cue 19 Go" (Go last).

| | |
|---|---|
| **Cut** | Describes an element of the show that has been removed or deleted. Often lines, scenic items, and light cues are "cut" from a production during the rehearsal process. |
| **Curtain Call** | At the end of a performance, the acknowledgement of applause by performers - the bows. |
| **Dead Case Storage** | Area to temporarily store empty road cases used to transport lighting, audio, A-V, or performer gear. |
| **Dolly** | A small wheeled platform used to move heavy items. |
| **Downstage** | 1. The stage area nearest the audience, also containing the apron.<br>2. A movement towards the audience. |
| **Drapes** | Stage curtains. |
| **Dress Rehearsal** | A full rehearsal, with all technical elements brought together. The performance as it will be "at the event." |
| **Dressing** | Decorative props added to a stage setting or an element of event décor are known as Set Dressing. |

| | |
|---|---|
| **Drop** | A hanging flat fabric piece, typically built of muslin and painted. |
| **Dry Run** | A practice run, usually a technical run without performers or key people. |
| **DSM** | Deputy Stage Manager. This is the member of the Stage Management team who attends all rehearsals and then calls the cues. Known in some places as a Stage Director or specifically for special events, the Technical Director. |
| **Duct Tape** | See Gaff Tape. |
| **Elevation** | A working drawing usually drawn to scale, showing the front view of a set, stage, event element or lighting rig. Nowadays, this drawing would be in CADD. |
| **Equity** | American Actor's Equity Association, founded in 1913, is the labor union representing actors and stage managers in the legitimate theater in the United States. |
| **Flat** | A timber frame usually covered with plywood or hardboard upon which are usually painted or designed scenic elements. Typical sizes are 4 ft wide x 8 ft high or 4 ft wide x 10 ft high. |
| **Fly** | To lift scenery, truss, luminaires, etc., into the air by support cables, chains, or ropes, with the aid of motors, pulleys, winches, and the like. |
| **Floor Plan** | A 2-D scale drawing of the event space in plan view. |
| **Foamcor** | A polystyrene, Styrofoam material used as a substrate for some reflector boards, or décor designs, effective because of its light weight and ease of mounting via reflector forks. |
| **Freight Elevator** | A specific-use elevator in a venue reserved for transporting technical and other equipment between floors. Typically, it is larger than a regular elevator, is located close to the loading bays and is accessible via service hallways. |
| **Front Curtain** | Located behind the proscenium, usually sewn with fullness, which serves as the prime closure between the auditorium and stage. Also known as proscenium curtain, house curtain, or grand drape. |
| **Front-Of-House (FOH)** | The complete area of the event space in front of the stage, (i.e. the audience area). |

| | |
|---|---|
| **Fullness** | Extra fabric sewn into pleats at the curtain tops. |
| **Gaff Tape** | Ubiquitous sticky cloth tape. Most common widths are .5 in. for marking out areas and 2 in. for everything else. It comes in a variety of colors and good decorators and event planners try to match the gaff tape color to the floor or carpet color. Used for temporarily securing almost anything. Should not be used on coiled cables or equipment. Also known as Duct Tape. |
| **Genie** | (Trade Name) A range of mobile access platforms with either hand-cranked or compressed air lifting mechanisms. |
| **Glitch** | 1. An unintended surge or brief interruption in an electrical current or signal. This can sometimes be detrimental to the integrity of the signal or to electronic equipment. |
| | 2. Any error in the execution of a cue. |
| **Glow Tape** | Luminous yellow self-adhesive tape used to mark floors and stair edges for safety and so that positions can be found in blackouts. |
| **Gooseneck** | A small work light, supplied with some control consoles and other equipment, that has a long, narrow, adjustable support, similar in appearance and mobility to the neck of a goose. They are usually removable and dimmable. |
| **Go** | The action word used by a Technical Director or DSM to cue other technical departments. |
| **Greasepaint** | Name refers to make-up supplied in stick form, for application to the face or body. Needs special removing cream. |
| **Green Room** | Changing room for performers. |
| **Ground Support** | The truss, lifts, and towers that are set up at ground, stage, or platform level and used to support other truss or equipment above. |
| **Headset** | 1. General term for theater/event communication equipment. |
| | 2. A headphone and microphone combination used in such communications systems with a beltpack. |
| **House Lighting** | Lighting control of the house separate from the stage lighting system, typical in all but the smallest venues. |

| | |
|---|---|
| **IATSE/I.A.T.S.E** | International Alliance of Theatrical Stage Employees (USA and Canada). Stage employees union. |
| **Kill** | 1. To switch off (a light/sound effect)<br>2. To strike/remove (a prop). |
| **Lift** | A height-adjustable stand or tower, sometimes motorized or operated with a crank mechanism or by gas or liquid pressure. |
| **Load In** | The process of moving all technical gear (e.g. audio, lighting, staging, décor) into a venue and setting it up prior to an event. |
| **Load Out** | The process of moving all technical gear out of a venue following an event. |
| **Loading Bay** | Parking access into a venue for unloading technical gear and décor. Usually close to a freight elevator. |
| **Marking Out** | Sticking tape to the floor of the stage to indicate the location of props, people, equipment, or direction of movement. |
| **Masking** | Neutral material or designed scenery that defines the performance area and conceals the technical areas. |
| **Marley** | Originally a brand name of a portable, non-slip vinyl covering used for dance performance. It has now come to be known more as a generic term for such a surface. There are several manufacturers of this type of surface. |
| **Offstage** | Out of sight from the audience. |
| **Onstage** | What happens in view of the audience on the stage. |
| **Open the House** | Clearance given to FOH staff by stage management that the stage is set and the audience can begin to take their seats. |
| **PM** | Short for Production Manager. |
| **Props** | (Short for Properties) Furnishings, set dressings, and all items large and small generally used as part of event décor. Usually separate from linens, murals, and all technical gear. |
| **Proscenium Arch** | Opening through which audience views a performance. Usually just called the proscenium, it is seldom actually arched in modern construction. |

| | |
|---|---|
| **Restore** | A cue to resume or return to any previous state, setting or function (e.g. lighting). |
| **Rider** | (Technical Rider) Information sent to a venue by a performance group detailing lighting, audio, staging, and dressing room requirements. Ideally arrives before the group! |
| **Risers** | Flat platforms of various sizes, usually portable, used for supporting luminaires or other production equipment, or sometimes used as portable stages. Standard sizes are 8 ft x 4 ft and 8 ft x 6 ft. Heights generally vary from 12 in. to 48 in. |
| **Road Case** | A sturdy, rugged box, often supplied with handles, and castors or wheels, used to transport and protect production equipment such as control consoles, dimmer racks, luminaires, and musical equipment. |
| **Sandbag** | Canvas bag used for weighing down scenery supports. |
| **Segue** (Pronounced "Segway") | Musical term for an immediate follow-on. Now often used as jargon for any kind of immediate follow-on in entertainment or event segments. |
| **Set** | A complete stage setting for a show or a complete piece of décor. |
| **Sight Lines** | Imaginary lines drawn from the most extreme seats in the house to the performing area to determine what portions of the performing area will be visible to all of the audience. |
| **Spike** | To mark the position of an item on stage, such as musical instruments, lecterns, and microphones. Spike tape is normally thin gaff tape, although other weaker tape (e.g. masking tape) is used on precious floors. |
| **Stage Crew** | Member of the stage staff who is responsible for moving props and/or scenery during the show, and for ensuring that items under their responsibility are working correctly and properly maintained. |
| **Stage Left** | The left side of the stage when facing the audience. |

| | |
|---|---|
| **Stage Light** | A luminaire intended to illuminate any portion of, or anything on, a stage or similar performing area, exclusive of practical lights and work lights. |
| **Stage Manager** | Person who assists with moving performers and equipment on and off stage. |
| **Stage Right** | The right side of the stage when facing the audience. |
| **Standby** | Audio cue for "Get Ready." |
| **Strike** | To remove all technical equipment and décor for storage and/or transport when an event is over. |
| **Travelers or Traveler Drape** | Curtains or scenic pieces moving on horizontal tracks. |
| **Talent** | Any and all performers. |
| **Upstage** | The part of the stage furthest from the audience. |
| **Visual Cue** | A cue taken by a technician from the action on stage rather than being cued by the stage manager or Technical Director. |
| **Wing** | The areas to the left and right of the stage or performing area not visible to the audience. Often set up as temporary areas and delineated with drape. |

Sample Form 20-1: Event Coordination Phase Check List

This phase begins once the sale is made and usually one month or more before the event.

## Risk Identification and Assessment

- ☐ Ensure all licenses and permits have been applied for and all insurance is in place.
- ☐ If a large public event, contact all fire, police, ambulance, first aid and security personnel/organizations to arrange for appropriate coverage and permits.
- ☐ Prepare emergency procedures for all above areas (fire, injury and first aid, security, police) as well as for lost children and lost and found.
- ☐ Identify traffic and crowd movement patterns and assess for potential risk. Make appropriate changes to plans and site/venue layout.
- ☐ Ensure signage is adequate and well–placed.
- ☐ Ensure disabled access is adequate for all event areas.

## Personnel Management

- ☐ Ensure all personnel (suppliers, venue, performers, other contractors) have all event details, including times, dates, schedules, location, and are aware of all the details of what they are providing.
- ☐ Ensure all personnel have proper attire and are aware of and following all regulations.
- ☐ Ensure all suppliers have contracts.

## Production Planning

- ☐ Re-confirm all event details with the client - date, location, number of people, demographics of guests, exact schedule, room, and any special requirements such as dress codes, performance times, speeches, and such.
- ☐ Call all suppliers and performers to confirm details of event.
- ☐ Call all suppliers and performers who were not chosen to release all holds on people or equipment.
- ☐ Contact venue to determine/confirm setup time, staging needs, electrical requirements (in detail, including cost), change room needs, load-in details, potential conflicting events during setup, room layout before and during event.

☐ Décor. Contact decorator and review event details. Work through the entire room/venue layout from start to finish. Ensure:

- o Decorations to be hung on walls have appropriate suspension mechanism. (e.g. no nails in walls, taped items will not fall, etc.)
- o Elements of decor suspended from ceiling can be hung easily, are not too heavy, and that appropriate ladders or lifts are available
- o Decor can be set up without hindering other setup of tables or room, or other changeovers
- o Scale of decor is going to be appropriate (i.e. Not too big for small room and not too small for big room)
- o Table centers will not interfere with sight lines
- o All three dimensions are considered equally. (i.e. Don't forget vertical dimension.)
- o Exits will not covered by décor
- o Lighting of all decor is planned and will be appropriate, adequate and easily accomplished
- o Florals are ordered
- o All decor and props are touched up, repaired and painted
- o All parts and tools will be ready and available (e.g. duct tape to match carpet color, bracing and enough sand bags for flats, returns for flats, complete tool kit, sufficient electrical extensions)
- o Transportation/truck is reserved
- o Staff/crew organized for setup and strike.

☐ Detailed (preferably computer-generated CADD) floor or site plan is completed and distributed to venue, client, decorators, performers, audio and lighting contractors, A-V contractor, and any others participating in event who need to know about it.

☐ Function Requirement Sheet with all details needed to be supplied from venue (or site) is completed and distributed to same people, and particularly venue.

☐ Entertainment. Contact all performers or their representatives and ensure:

- o All contract riders and special contract details for name acts are reviewed for possible problems or excessive costs
- o All special requirements are appropriate and can be available (e.g. certain stage

surface, certain sound needs, etc.)

o   Appropriate stage size ordered (note that a performance in a large room for large audience generally needs a 32 in. stage height or more, a dance band stage only needs a 12 or 16 in. stage height)

o   Changing room will be available and will be close to stage area if necessary

o   Rehearsal scheduled if needed

o   Costuming/attire will be appropriate (e.g. no jeans)

o   All performance times, lengths of performances, and details are passed to performers

o   Whatever power, audio or lights needed will be provided by the client or the performer

o   Schedule passed to performers for setup and for entire event

o   All necessary details are included on performers' contracts, including date, time, location and directions to venue if necessary

o   Performers know that prices are not to be discussed with client and that all future requests for their services are to come through the planner if a result of this particular event

o   Planner's business cards are made available to performers to hand out. No personal cards or phone numbers are to be given out

o   Sufficient stage managers are booked and budgeted for.

☐   Sound/Lights/Audio Visual. Review all initial proposals and ensure/determine:

o   Sound will be adequate for audience size

o   If speeches will be necessary, is podium, podium mic, wireless or handheld mic needed

o   Sound is appropriate for room acoustics and purpose of event. (e.g. Distributed or delay speakers for large room, only speakers near stage for just a band, flown speakers for best sound quality, classiness and visibility, but higher price, etc.)

o   Best location for console

o   Size of system coming

o   Cassette/CD player available with tapes/CDs as needed.  Always useful if unexpected walk-in music or background music requested at last minute

o   Sufficient cabling and mats for doorways or walkway areas planned

o   Sufficient staffing planned

o   Crew breaks planned into schedule

o   Floor plan and schedule passed to audio, lighting and A-V companies

o   Adequate lighting for stage, room and/or decor planned

o   Followspots ordered if needed

o   Location of lighting trees and/or speakers will not interfere with walkways or with sight lines

o   If lights will be flown. If so, can they be flown with sound system

o   Sufficient power is ordered, electrician will be available if necessary, cost is taken into consideration in budget

o   Lighting console is co-located with audio console if possible

o   Correct screen size(s) is ordered for A-V

o   All slides, videos and format, computer shows, etc. are passed to A-V company in detail

o   Adequate space is allowed for rear-screen A-V presentations if requested

o   A-V company is given schedule and floor plan

o   A-V console is integrated with others if possible

o   That an overall Technical Director will be present at the event to "call the show" if needed

o   Sufficient intercom equipment (i.e. Radios, Clear-Com, etc.) is ordered for all technical personnel as needed.

☐   Catering. Address the following, especially if you are subcontracting the caterer:

o   Confirm number of courses and any special requirements or needs that might affect the outcome or running of the event. For example, if warmers will be used on a buffet which might affect the total power required if it has to be shared with lighting.

o   Ensure that there is sufficient space for catering to serve diners and for your event entertainment, décor and other equipment to fit into the venue.

o   If catered by an outside caterer, ensure all equipment, including serving tables, preparation area, cleanup area, guest tables, chairs, cutlery and staff are adequate and appropriate for number of guests.

o   Ensure that caterer's schedule agrees with yours. Avoid any potential setup interference by adjusting schedules.

o   Ensure that all food will be served in its proper condition (e.g. no chance of hot meals NOT being hot).

o   Ensure special meals (e.g. vegetarian) are planned and in correct numbers.

## Contracting

- ☐ Complete all bookings and contracts for client and suppliers. Ensure contracts are signed and sent out with all details.  Double check that correct deposit is requested and that client knows amount required and when it is due.
- ☐ Follow up to ensure all contracts are signed and returned on schedule, and that deposits are received (or sent out to suppliers) in accordance with contract(s).

Sample Form 20-2:  Event Execution Phase Check List

This phase usually begins approximately two days before the event and ends after strike.

## Risk Management

- ☐ Ensure appropriate insurance, licenses and permits are in place with either you or other suppliers.
- ☐ Double check event site or venue for appropriate signage, easy crowd control including access and exit.
- ☐ Ensure emergency procedures are written and copies are distributed to all event personnel.
- ☐ Ensure emergency and security personnel are in place.
- ☐ Ensure all personnel have appropriate safety clothing and that those who must operate specialized equipment (e.g. Genie lift) are qualified.
- ☐ Check site or venue to ensure:

  - o All exits and evacuation routes are clear
  - o Stage stairs and edges are marked with safety tape
  - o Stage stairs have hand rails
  - o Electrical boxes are marked with caution signs
  - o All cabling crossing foot traffic areas is securely matted and taped down
  - o Lighting is at safe levels
  - o All flown trussing, audio, lighting, A-V, décor and other equipment has been adequately secured and is safe
  - o All elevators are working
  - o All foot traffic routes are large enough to accommodate the number of people planned (e.g. routes to the stage for performers)
  - o No decor or other equipment presents any danger to guests or others.

## Personnel Management

- ☐ Ensure you have all supplier emergency contact information (work, home, and cell phone numbers).
- ☐ Ensure all suppliers and performers are aware of load in and setup locations and re-

strictions (e.g. scheduling at loading dock, distances from load-in to event location/ room, other conflicting meetings or events, exactly who to report to at venue and where to find that person).

- ☐ Check supplier attire.
- ☐ Ensure proper equipment is available for suppliers, either provided by them (e.g. tools) or by another source (e.g. genie lift from the venue).
- ☐ Prior to start of setup and periodically throughout setup, review and monitor schedule for problem areas and to ensure everyone is on time.

## Production Management

- ☐ Two days before event, call all performers and suppliers to ensure everything is ready and all are familiar with the schedule. Also double check contact names and phone numbers. Have them handy for the event.
- ☐ Dress appropriately for event (Jacket/tie, suit or dress for women). Don't forget your name tag.
- ☐ Bring all event papers, especially contact phone numbers, and keep them handy.
- ☐ Arrive at venue early or if decor, audio, lights, or A-V are first, arrive in sufficient time to check for mistakes and have them corrected.
- ☐ Immediately on arrival, contact client and venue to let them know you are present and available for consultation.
- ☐ Re-check schedule with client plus any unusual additions such as speeches or special presentations. Also determine where client will be in case you must get in touch with him in a hurry.
- ☐ Walk entire event setup several times to ensure all decor, audio, lights, A-V, staging, changing rooms, are as promised and as planned.
- ☐ Liaise with venue staff member in charge and relay any items that will affect his/her staff such as performances or speeches in between meal courses and such. If possible and budget permits, try to get refreshments (limited) for crew and/or performers.
- ☐ Greet performers as they arrive and show them to their dressing rooms. Be friendly.
- ☐ On with the show!! Adhere to schedules as much as possible. Have performers or speakers ready to be onstage at least 10 minutes before they are scheduled. (Note the more detailed section in this book about Stage Management and Calling a Show).
- ☐ After event, thank suppliers, performers and client. Ask client if everything went as expected and can we be of service again. Pay performers or suppliers as required.

## Contract Management

- ☐ Pay all suppliers promptly, preferably at the event if possible.
- ☐ If client has not paid final installment, request immediate payment prior to event or determine and agree on the final payment method and timing. Send a confirming e-mail or letter immediately following the event if payment is not paid in full at the event. This will also enable a review of any additional items or changes to the contract made onsite, which may not have been able to be confirmed in writing.

# Part Six

# Event Evolution:
# The Followup Phase

# 21

# How to Follow Up

This phase of the event immediately follows the end of the event itself. It is a step that is all too often forgotten. The good, professional planner would do well to remember that a little followup goes a long way to showing your dedication to working in the client's best interest.

At the very least, if the event is not complicated or you have not had the opportunity to meet the client face-to-face, a phone call should be made to the client the day after the event in order to receive feedback, good or bad. At the same time, and preferably before the call to the client, a call should be made to all suppliers to ensure that the event was executed according to their contract and that there were no problems. If there were, it gives you the opportunity to know at least one side of the story before you talk to the client. If there were major problems - and one never wants nor plans for these - then the supplier calls enable you to consider appropriate corrective action or at least allow you to provide some explanation to your client. The client call is important because it establishes that you are truly interested in the product and service you offer and are willing to do whatever it takes to make it better.

If the event is one that is repeated on a regular basis such as an annual awards show or banquet or festival, then the entire event team should assemble and each member should complete a debrief of what was successful, what was unsuccessful, what could be eliminated, what could be added, and what could be improved. Followup actions with target dates and persons responsible should be created and monitored for completion.

Followup action also entails invoicing the client and receiving all payments according to your contract. These accounts receivable should be strictly followed and not allowed to go over 30 days.

In addition to invoicing and phoning, a formal thank-you is usually in order. This can be done best with the combination of a letter and evaluation sheet which can be e-mailed, faxed, or mailed back to you. This is a great method of also scouting new leads and determining when is the best time to call this client back for future events for which you may also be a part. We have designed an evaluation letter that enables us to ask how we did and also to ask for information about future events (see Sample Form 21-1).

One final but often overlooked step in followup is to also talk to the venue where the event was held. In many cases this will be a hotel or similar location. It is a good idea to contact the Catering Manager or Conference Services Manager to ascertain if everything went well from their side. In some cases, the event may have been fabulous from your point of view and from the client's point of view, but a minor glitch or perhaps argument or even damage might have occurred during the event strike and might have become overblown depending on whose side of the story is being told. If this is not addressed through contact with the venue, you may never know about it and may wonder why you are "persona non grata" at that establishment in the future. Always try to contact the key person at the venue.

Sample Form 21-1: Event Evaluation Form

## EVENT EVALUATION

Thank you for allowing ABC Event Company Ltd. to be a part of your event. In our continuing effort to present the best shows possible, we value your opinions and comments. Therefore, we would appreciate your taking the time to complete the enclosed evaluation form and to fax or mail it back to us at the number/address below. We will keep all information confidential.

Name: _____ Organization: _____

Event Date:_____Event Type: _____

Please rate the following elements from 1 (poor) to 5 (excellent) by circling the appropriate number:

| | | | | | | |
|---|---|---|---|---|---|---|
| 1. | Speedy service regarding pricing and proposals | 1 | 2 | 3 | 4 | 5 |
| 2. | Creativity of suggestions | 1 | 2 | 3 | 4 | 5 |
| 3. | Competitive pricing | 1 | 2 | 3 | 4 | 5 |
| 4. | Entertainment. Appropriate and professional | 1 | 2 | 3 | 4 | 5 |
| 5. | Décor. Creativity, quality, appropriate to theme, quantity | 1 | 2 | 3 | 4 | 5 |
| 6. | Event execution. Attention to details, liaison with facility, smoothness of show and all elements of event | 1 | 2 | 3 | 4 | 5 |
| 7. | Coordination of catering, A-V, sound, | | | | | |

|  | lighting, staging, etc. | 1 | 2 | 3 | 4 | 5 |

8. Hotel and site selection (where applicable)     1    2    3    4    5

9. Business meeting production and support
   (where applicable)     1    2    3    4    5

Comments:_____

_____

_____

_____

_____

_____

May we contact you or another person responsible for the next important event for your organization?

Name:_____Phone: _____

Fax: _____E-mail: _____

Date of Next Event: _____

City/State (Province)/Country of Next Event: _____

_____

Can you recommend us to at least two other organizations that could use our company's services?

1. Name: _____Phone: _____
   Address: _____

2. Name: _____Phone: _____
   Address: _____

Thank you for your feedback. Please mail or fax this form back to:

**ABC Event Company Ltd.**
**1234 Main St.**
**Vancouver, BC V4R 5T7 Canada**
**Fax: 123-456-7890**
**Phone: 123-567-8901**
**E-mail: info@abceventcompany.com**

Sample Form 21-2: Event Followup Phase Check List

This phase begins immediately after the event itself and ends when the client has paid the bill! The day after the event, the following should be started:

- ☐ Call all suppliers to double check that they were happy with the outcome of the event.
- ☐ Call the appropriate contact person (e.g. Conference Services Manager or Catering Manager) at the venue to check that they were happy with the outcome of the event.
- ☐ Call the client to ensure they were happy with the event and to double check and agree on any contractual additions or deletions.
- ☐ Ensure any extra costs are added to the total budget and a final invoice sent to the client along with a thank you letter and Event Evaluation Form.
- ☐ Send out a thank you card (handwritten) or letter (typed) to the client as soon as possible after the event. If a small event, ensure that at least a standard form letter is sent out with the evaluation sheet.
- ☐ Make a note on your calendar to call the client six months prior to the event next year to request if you can be of service if the event is an annual one.
- ☐ Follow up immediately on any leads given to you as a result of the event.
- ☐ Track accounts receivable religiously until they are paid and try to keep them less than 30 days.

# Part Seven

# References and Industry Information

Fortunately, as the experience level of event planners grows each year, there are more and more resources becoming available where extensive knowledge can be found.

Although far from an exhaustive list, most of the main books, magazines, and organizations, plus several key web sites are listed below.

# BOOKS

- *The Business of Event Planning: Behind-the-Scenes Secrets of Successful Special Events*, by Judy Allen (Author), Publisher: John Wiley & Sons; 1st edition (September 16, 2002), ISBN: 047083188X
- *A Passion for Parties: Your Guide to Elegant Entertaining*, by David Tutera, Laura Morton, Publisher: Simon & Schuster; (September 18, 2001), ISBN: 0743202287
- *The International Dictionary of Event Management*, by Joe Goldblatt (Editor), Kathleen S. Nelson (Editor), Publisher: John Wiley & Sons; 2nd edition (January 2001), ISBN: 047139453X
- *Gala!: The Special Event Planner for Professionals and Volunteers*, by Patti Coons, Patti Coons, Publisher: Capital Books Inc; (December 20, 1999), ISBN: 1892123134
- *Dollars & Events: How to Succeed in the Special Events Business*, by Joe Goldblatt (Author), Frank Supovitz (Author), Publisher: John Wiley & Sons; (March 1999), ISBN: 0471249572
- *Affairs of the Heart: How to Start and Operate a Successful Special Event Planning Service*, by Nancy DeProspo, Publisher: Nancy Deprospo Limited; Ringbound edition (July 1993), ISBN: 0963808508
- *Special Events: Best Practices in Modern Event Management*, by Joe Jeff Goldblatt, Publisher: John Wiley & Sons; 2nd edition (December 1997), ASIN: 0471287458
- *Behind the Scenes at Special Events: Flowers, Props, and Design*, by Lena Malouf (Author), Publisher: John Wiley & Sons; (January 1999), ISBN: 0471254916
- *Pick a Party: The Big Book of Party Themes and Occasions*, by Patty Sachs, Publisher: Meadowbrook; (September 1997), ISBN: 0671521233
- *Themes, Dreams, and Schemes: Banquet Menu Ideas, Concepts, and Thematic Experiences*, by G. Eugene Wigger (Author), Publisher: John Wiley & Sons; (June 1997), ISBN: 0471153915
- *Event Management & Event Tourism*, by Donald Getz, Publisher: Cognizant Communication Corp; (June 1997), ISBN: 188234510X
- *The Art of the Party: Design Ideas for Successful Entertaining*, by Renny Reynolds,

Elaine Louie (Contributor), Edward Addeo (Photographer), Publisher: Penguin Studio; (August 1992) , ASIN: 0670830542

- *Special Events: Inside and Out*, by Steven Wood Schmader, Robert Jackson, Publisher: Sagamore Publishing, Inc.; 2nd edition (September 1997), ISBN: 1571671285
- *Black Tie Optional: The Ultimate Guide to Planning and Producing Successful Special Events*, by Harry A. Freedman, Karen Feldman Smith, Harry A. Freeman, Publisher: Taft Group; (November 1994), ASIN: 0930807170
- *The Complete Guide to Special Event Management: Business Insights, Financial Advice, and Successful Strategies from Ernst & Young, Advisors to the Olympics, the Emmy Awards and the PGA Tour*, by Ernst & Young LLP (Author), Dwight W. Catherwood (Author), Richard L. Van Kirk (Author), Publisher: John Wiley & Sons; (May 1992), ISBN: 0471549088
- *The Art of Event Design*, by Liese Gardner, Joe Atlas (Photographer), Susan Terpening (Photographer), Liese, C. Gardner, Nadine Froger, Susan, E Terpening, Publisher: Intertec/Miramar Communications; 1 edition (January 7, 1998), ASIN: 0966170105
- *Event Planning: The Ultimate Guide to Successful Meetings, Corporate Events, Fundraising Galas, Conferences, Conventions, Incentives and Other Special Events*, by Judy Allen, Publisher: Wiley, John & Sons, Incorporated, May 2000, ISBN: 0471644129
- *Managing Special Event Risks: 10 Steps to Safety*, by Nonprofit Risk Management Center, Nonprofits' Insurance Alliance of California, Publisher: Non Profit Risk Management; 1 edition (November 1, 1997), ISBN: 0963712047
- *Complete Idiot's Guide to Meeting and Event Planning*, by Robin E Craven, Lynn Johnson Golabowski, Lynn Johnson Golabowski, Robin E Craven, Publisher: Alpha Books; 1st edition (March 19, 2001), ISBN: 0028640047
- *Creating Special Events: The Ultimate Guide*, by Linda Surbeck, Jack Jefferies (Illustrator), Publisher: Master of Ceremonies; (June 1990), ISBN: 0962882003
- *Special Events: Twenty-First Century Global Event Management*, by Joe Goldblatt (Author), Publisher: John Wiley & Sons; 3rd edition (December 2001), ISBN: 0471396877
- *The Fundraising Manual: A Step by Step Guide to Creating the Perfect Event*, by Micki Gordon, Publisher: FIG Press; (July 1997), ISBN: 0964929937
- *Lateral Thinking: Creativity Step by Step*, by Edward de Bono, Publisher: Harper & Row, 1990, ISBN: 0-06-090325-2

# MAGAZINES

- *Canadian Event Perspective.* News magazine focused on the business of the Canadian events and meetings industry. This glossy, tabloid style publication delivers the news, the issues, and the facts about this dynamic industry. You'll find special interest stories; business news; discussions about topics that affect the industry; the latest tidbits on Canadian companies; unique profiles on the hottest movers and shakers in the industry; venue reviews; career news; classifieds; association news; entertainment and talent happenings; a national events calendar and more! www.canadianspecialevents.com/CEP/home.html

- *Corporate & Incentive Travel.* Corporate & Incentive Travel magazine is read by over 40,000 ABC audited meeting and incentive travel planners and key executives responsible for meeting decisions. Articles range monthly from in-depth how-to's, to issue-oriented features, examinations of professional concerns, thoroughly researched destination reports, and columns by industry experts. www.corporate-inc-travel.com

- *Corporate Meetings and Incentives.* Corporate Meetings & Incentives is a monthly magazine that explores trends in management and motivation as they relate to companies successfully communicating with employees through meetings, and driving performance through incentive programs. Readers are 36,000 senior executives who make the decisions on their companies' off-site meetings and incentive programs. Circulation is qualified, so you must answer a list of questions to receive the magazine. www.meetingsnet.com

- *Event Solutions.* Through Event Solutions magazine, readers get information on all aspects of the event industry. With emphasis on overall event production and events with significant impact, readers are able to keep their fingers on the pulse of this ever-changing industry. Event Solutions is read by more than 25,000 event professionals, who include corporate and association planners, in addition to independent producers, event sites, technical producers, designers, decorators, caterers, event rentals, and more. www.event-solutions.com

- *Incentive Magazine.* Incentive is the only publication devoted exclusively to motivation and performance improvement through the use of incentive programs and consumer promotions. We are a FIRST-READ for executives looking to improve company performance and a FIRST-BUY for advertisers looking to reach the most qualified incentive buyer decision-makers. www.incentivemag.com/incentive/about_

us/index.jsp

- *Meeting Professional.* The Meeting Professional is mailed monthly to nearly 20,000 MPI members and 11,500 qualified nonmember meeting industry planners. It is also distributed at major industry shows, such as ASAE, ITME, EIBTM, MPI conferences and upon individual request. The circulation includes 11,500 MPI qualified meeting planners and incentive planners. www.mpiweb.org/news/tmp

- *Meetings & Conventions.* M&C publishes a variety of articles on topics of interest to meeting planners, corporate travel personnel, travel agents, trade show managers, incentive planners, and other members of the hospitality industry. www.meetings-conventions.com

- *Meetings Canada.* Meetings & Incentive Travel Magazine is the leading publication in Canada targeting Canadian meeting, conference, exposition and incentive travel managers. www.bizlink.com/meetingscanada.htm

- *Special Events Magazine.* The publication serves as a resource for event professionals who design and produce special events including social, corporate and public events held in hotels, resorts, banquet facilities and other venues. *Special Events Magazine* offers a comprehensive, behind-the-scenes analysis of events from the professional's perspective while providing solutions on design and menu inspiration, sales-building strategies, business management tips and more www.specialevents.com

- *Successful Meetings.* Edited for meeting planners across all industries, Successful Meetings features articles on thought-provoking and timely issues. It covers innovative ways to motivate a staff; the "how to" sections give specific ideas and techniques to get better results from meetings, and site and destination updates help evaluate meeting facilities and destinations to get the most value for the money. www.successmtgs.com/successmtgs/index.jsp

- *Tradeshow Week Magazine.* For the past 31 years, Tradeshow Week has focused on the entire tradeshow industry with a commitment to providing tradeshow professionals with the latest information they need to perform their jobs more efficiently and effectively. www.tradeshowweek.com

# ORGANIZATIONS

- *CAEM (Canadian Association of Exposition Managers).* Canada's national association of professional show producers, show managers, and industry suppliers. They provide valuable industry-specific services, programs and products, including a newsletter, unique publications, employment referral, seminars, an annual conference, professional certification and industry research. www.caem.ca

- *CSES (Canadian Special Events Society).* A Canadian association representing the Special Events Industry in Canada. www.cses.ca
- *IAEM (International Association of Exposition Managers).* The premier association for all individuals with business interests in the exhibition industry. Today IAEM represents over 3,500 individuals who conduct and support exhibitions around the world. www.iaem.org
- *IAFE (International Association of Fairs and Expositions).* The International Association of Fairs and Expositions (IAFE) is a voluntary, non-profit corporation organizing state, district, and county agricultural fairs, state and provincial associations of fairs, expositions, associations, corporations, and individuals into one large association interested in the improvement of fairs and allied fields. www.fairsandexpos.com
- *IFEA (International Festivals and Events Association).* The International Festival and Events Association has provided cutting-edge professional development and fund-raising ideas to the special events industry for 45 years. Through publications, seminars, the annual convention & trade show, and ongoing networking, IFEA is advancing festivals and events throughout the world. www.ifea.com
- *IMPAC (Independent Meeting Planners Association of Canada).* IMPAC was formed in 1996 to provide a forum for entrepreneurs in the meetings, conference and event planning profession to meet, share ideas, gain new and valuable information on the industry and work together to form a strong presence in the marketplace. www.impaccanada.com
- *ISES (International Special Events Society).* The Mission of ISES is to educate, advance and promote the special events industry and its network of professionals along with related industries. www.ises.com
- *MPI (Meeting Professionals International).* Established in 1972, Meeting Professionals International (MPI) is the leading global community committed to shaping and defining the future of the meeting and event industry. MPI helps its members enhance their professional value by providing them with best practices, superior education, the latest research and trends, professional development and networking opportunities. www.mpiweb.org
- *NACE (National Association of Catering Executives).* The NACE mission is to assist caterers in achieving career success by raising the level of education

and professionalism of the catering industry. www.nace.net

- *PCMA (Professional Convention Management Association).* The Professional Convention Management Association (PCMA) is a nonprofit international association of professionals in the meetings industry whose mission is to deliver breakthrough education and promote the value of professional convention management. www.pcma.org
- *SITE (Society of Incentive Travel Executives).* The Society of Incentive & Travel Executives is a worldwide organization of business professionals dedicated to the recognition and development of motivational and performance improvement strategies of which travel is a key component. It recognizes the global cultural differences and practices in developing these strategies, and serves as a networking and educational opportunity for its m++embers. www.site-intl.org
- *WAEM (Western Association of Exhibition Management).* The Western Association of Exhibition Management is a non-profit society of individuals and organizations that are directly concerned with the management, planning and production of special events, conferences and trade and consumer exhibitions of all sizes. To further its objectives and to protect consumers, members, abide by a strict code of professional principles that govern the conduct and maintain the reputation of the association. www.waem.org

# OTHER USEFUL WEB SITES

- http://www.corbinball.com/. One of the most comprehensive web sites devoted to anything concerning meeting planning and special events, with hundreds of links to other sites.
- http://www.expoworld.net/. A major portal for industry knowledge, including festivals and events, courses, and company searches.
- http://www.theatrecrafts.com/. Excellent resource full of glossaries for all technical areas and theatre terminology. Lots of resource books also available.
- http://bizbash.com/. Wonderful site devoted to mostly New York events but content-rich with other useful event information.
- http://www.alss1.com/. Very good glossaries on audio and lighting equipment.
- http://sen5es.com/. Excellent site by Senses Catering chock full of useful information on catering.
- http://unitedvisual.com/. Very good resource for information on A-V technology.

- http://thewritingworks.com/index.html. Nice site with quite a lot of useful information and ideas for the meetings industry and events.
- http://law.freeadvice.com/. Excellent site for free legal advice, including contract law.
- http://mylegalanswers.com/. More legal advice, particularly Canadian.
- http://www.edwdebono.com/index.html. Web site of noted creativity expert Edward de Bono.
- http://tentexperts.org. Site provided by the Tent Rental Division of the Industrial Fabrics Association International, with lots of information and references about using tents.
- http://www.canadianspecialevents.com. Site for all things to do with the Canadian Special Events Industry, including the highly successful Canadian Special Events and Meetings Expo, a trade show and educational conference held annually in major Canadian cities.

# Endnotes

1   Baragona, John (January 2003 ). <u>Event Solutions Magazine – 2003 Fact Book</u>, 24-34

2   De Bono, Edward, (1970) <u>Lateral Thinking - Creativity Step by Step</u>, New York, NY: Harper & Row

3   Ibid. Baragona, John (January 2003). <u>Event Solutions Magazine – 2003 Fact Book</u>. 32

4   Steve Matthews, Show Time Lighting, Vancouver, BC, Canada (personal communications, March 2003)

5   Patil, Ajay, Rabbitt, Jay, Waldrop, Doc (2000, August). <u>Act I: Scene II – "Lighting & Sound Elements"</u>. Presentation at Event Solutions Magazine Expo 2000, Atlanta, Georgia, USA

6   Goldblatt, Dr. Joe, CSEP (2002). <u>Special Events, Third Edition</u>, NewYork: John Wiley & Sons, Inc.

7   Dunn, Barbara, (2000, August). <u>Legal Ease</u>. Presentation at Event Solutions Magazine 5th Annual Expo 2001, St. Louis, MO, USA

8   Knight, Bill, (2002, August). <u>Risk Management</u>. Presentation at Event Solutions Magazine 6th Annual Expo, Miami Beach, FL, USA

9   Watts/Lapointe, (2002). <u>Risk Management for Special Events.</u> Notes for Continuing Education Department of Capilano College, North Vancouver, BC, Canada, 2002 Workshop

10  Daly, Sheryl, (2001, April). <u>Contracts Pertaining to the Performing Arts</u>. Paper presented at Pacific Contact 2001, Burnaby, BC, Canada, sponsored by the BC Touring Council for the Performing Arts.

11  Quick, Terry, (2001, August). <u>Understanding Contracts</u>, Presentation at Event Solutions Magazine 5th Annual Expo 2001, St. Louis, MO, USA

CPSIA information can be obtained
at www.ICGtesting.com
Printed in the USA
LVHW020109130319
610430LV00006B/19/P

9 781425 128029